Educational Theory of the Unforeseen

Also Available from Bloomsbury

Education, Equality and Justice in the New Normal, edited by Inny Accioly and Donaldo Macedo

Peace Education, edited by Monisha Bajaj and Maria Hantzopoulos

Echoes from Freire for a Critically Engaged Pedagogy, Peter Mayo

On Critical Pedagogy, Henry A. Giroux

Pedagogy, Politics and Philosophy of Peace: Interrogating Peace and Peacemaking, edited by Carmel Borg and Michael Grech

Politics and Pedagogy in the 'Post-Truth' Era: Insurgent Philosophy and Praxis, Derek R. Ford

Postdigital Dialogues on Critical Pedagogy, Liberation Theology and Information Technology, Peter McLaren and Petar Jandric

Race, Education and Educational Leadership in England, edited by Paul Miller and Christine Callender

Race, Politics and Pandemic Pedagogy: Education in a Time of Crisis, Henry A. Giroux

Transnational Perspectives on Democracy, Citizenship, Human Rights and Peace Education, edited by Mary Drinkwater, Fazal Rizvi and Karen Edge

Educational Theory of the Unforeseen

Educating for an Unpredictable Future

Herner Saeverot and Glenn-Egil Torgersen

BLOOMSBURY ACADEMIC
LONDON • NEW YORK • OXFORD • NEW DELHI • SYDNEY

BLOOMSBURY ACADEMIC
Bloomsbury Publishing Plc
50 Bedford Square, London, WC1B 3DP, UK
1385 Broadway, New York, NY 10018, USA
29 Earlsfort Terrace, Dublin 2, Ireland

BLOOMSBURY, BLOOMSBURY ACADEMIC and the
Diana logo are trademarks of Bloomsbury Publishing Plc

First published in Great Britain 2024

Copyright © Herner Saeverot and Glenn-Egil Torgersen, 2024

Herner Saeverot and Glenn-Egil Torgersen have asserted their right under the Copyright, Designs and Patents Act, 1988, to be identified as Authors of this work.

For legal purposes the Acknowledgements on p. x constitute an extension of this copyright page.

Cover design by Grace Ridge

This work is published open access subject to a Creative Commons Attribution-NonCommercial-NoDerivatives 4.0 International licence (CC BY-NC-ND 4.0, https://creativecommons.org/licenses/by-nc-nd/4.0/). You may re-use, distribute, and reproduce this work in any medium for non-commercial purposes, provided you give attribution to the copyright holder and the publisher and provide a link to the Creative Commons licence.

Bloomsbury Publishing Plc does not have any control over, or responsibility for, any third-party websites referred to or in this book. All internet addresses given in this book were correct at the time of going to press. The author and publisher regret any inconvenience caused if addresses have changed or sites have ceased to exist, but can accept no responsibility for any such changes.

A catalogue record for this book is available from the British Library.

A catalog record for this book is available from the Library of Congress.

ISBN: HB: 978-1-3503-5605-4
PB: 978-1-3503-5606-1
ePDF: 978-1-3503-5607-8
eBook: 978-1-3503-5608-5

Typeset by Integra Software Services Pvt. Ltd.
Printed and bound in Great Britain

To find out more about our authors and books visit www.bloomsbury.com and sign up for our newsletters.

Contents

List of Figures		vi
List of Tables		vii
Preface		viii
Acknowledgements		x
1	Educating and Researching for What Is Not Yet Known	1
2	A Brief History of Pedagogy of the Unforeseen	23
3	Existential Education and the Unforeseen	37
4	Pedagogical Practice and Improvisation under Unforeseen Circumstances	51
5	Didactic Models for the Unforeseen	71
6	The Unforeseen and New Forms of Terrorism	91
7	Teaching the Unknown, or How Teachers Can Prepare Students for Uncertainty	103
References		113
Index		119

Figures

1.1 Didactic Bow-tie model 12
5.1 Degree of the unforeseen 75
5.2 Strategic didactic TU model 77
5.3 Didactic Balance Model 88

Tables

1.1 Overview of nuanced differences in expression of the unforeseen (TU) in relation to risks and dangers (modified after Kvernbekk, Torgersen & Moe, 2015)   5

5.1 Overview of the content and meaning of the various didactic categories in an expanded didactic relation model for education, as a basis for didactic decisions related to the unforeseen (the outer circle in Figure 5.2) (modified after Torgersen & Saeverot, 2015)   78

5.2 Competency structures in the category 'Knowledge Competency' (modified after Torgersen & Saeverot, 2015)   82

5.3 Competency structures in the category 'No Knowledge' (modified after Torgersen & Saeverot, 2015)   84

5.4 Competency structures in the category 'Tiers of Unforeseeability' (modified after Torgersen & Saeverot, 2015)   85

Preface

Based on the Chernobyl accident in 1986, the German sociologist Ulrich Beck (1944–2015) formulated the term 'risk society'. By that he meant that all citizens, in all types of society, can be exposed to threats that cannot be easily neutralized. Therefore, we must all be on guard so that we can be aware of danger signals that can help us to meet unforeseen events and situations in fruitful manners. We need to know what is actually happening. At the same time, Beck underlined that neither politicians nor the individual citizens must resort to the extreme; viz., to develop fear and paranoia, where almost everything is perceived as dangerous and threatening. Researchers, politicians, the media and others have a great responsibility here. Be it small or large societies, we must be able to prepare for crises, where hope shines through our narratives, without fear taking over.

Here it may be appropriate to mention that the concept of the unforeseen has a Janus face. On the one hand, it can create space for productive moments with the potential to learn and gain new insights. On the other hand, it can lead to destructive consequences. In particular, the school has an important role in both of these possible outcomes. Imagine that you are teaching a class in the fifth year of primary school. Suddenly you have to leave the class to take care of a situation and when you return to the classroom, several desks have been deliberately destroyed by some students. Or imagine a more positive example where you are teaching a ninth-grade class, when suddenly one of the students, completely unexpectedly, claims that you are wrong in what you are conveying. What does one do in such situations? Catching moments, improvising, becoming aware of one's own experiences and being able to use emerging situations as potential for learning in teaching can be seen as examples of making use of unforeseen situations.

Although there is not one and right solution to what one should do in such situations, one of the points in this book is that teachers who have pedagogical preparedness in advance will be able to cope with unknown situations and utilize this in pedagogical practice better than teachers who do not have insight in the nature of the unforeseen.

Although the book is scientific in its form and based on many years of systematic and basic research, we will also emphasize what educators can do to create a safe learning environment, even in an unpredictable world. This challenges traditional curriculum theory and learning theory, and both teachers and students will find themselves in this tension. In this book, we will therefore give examples of solutions based on basic pedagogical research in and on pedagogical practice. We also aim to provide knowledge about what educators need to know in order to be able to implement a pedagogy that takes account of the unforeseen.

Having said that, we encourage the readers of this book to further develop our knowledge and theory of a pedagogy of the unforeseen. With this, we hope that the unforeseen can be part of the agenda in the discipline of education, teacher education programmes, curriculum thinking and education policy, so that the citizens of the future can meet and deal with the unforeseen in the most appropriate ways possible, including facilitating and exploiting productive moments during both dangerous and non-dangerous situations when it comes to learning for the good of individuals and society. More research is needed in and on pedagogy of the unforeseen.

This book has been written by us with equal effort and contribution.
Oslo, January 2024
Herner Saeverot and *Glenn-Egil Torgersen*

Acknowledgements

Capitalism, war, malicious intelligence, pandemics, climate change, loss of biological diversity and distortions of the truth are examples of existential threats that threaten our quality of life and freedom, and even democracy itself. When we humans are threatened, we are naturally concerned about how to meet and mitigate this threat. Nevertheless, both people and organizations can be locked into existing concepts, mental maps and practices in such a way that they are unable to handle the unexpected or the unknown in effective ways. This was one of the reasons why we in 2008 started to work systematically with a research project on pedagogy and the unforeseen.

We sat in a boat, in a safe harbour, and gradually arrived at one of the most pressing challenges and research questions in educational theory and practice: Is it possible to learn and practice something that is not yet known? To this we connected threats and preparedness, but also more positive approaches from pedagogy, such as learning and being cultivated as a person (in German: *Bildung*).

To take it a step further, we set out on an interdisciplinary path with over fifty researchers from all over the world. This is how we introduced the concept and the phenomenon of 'existential threats', within a pedagogical framework, which we referred to as 'pedagogy of the unforeseen'. We hereby wish to thank all our collaborators and fellow researchers who have helped to develop knowledge and theory when it comes to pedagogy of the unforeseen. Without them, this project would not have been possible.

We wish to thank Mark Richardson at Bloomsbury for his encouragement and commitment to our project, and also Elissa Burns at Bloomsbury for her good help and support along the way. We are also grateful to our institutions, Western Norway University and University of South-Eastern Norway, for financing the Open Access book. We would also like to thank the anonymous reviewers for helpful suggestions and remarks, and the proofreaders for improving the language.

1
Educating and Researching for What Is Not Yet Known

The core message and goals of the book

Many events, both destructive and constructive, occur unexpectedly to various government agencies and actors. At the same time, sudden events that occur, for example, in life in general, be it in the kindergarten, the classroom, the lecture hall, in a guidance situation or at the workplace, can also mean something nice, positive, joyful and rich in learning – if this is captured and utilized into something positive and for learning. However, common to both unforeseen dangerous and positive events is that we who experience this do not know what is coming or what this means for the near future, or perhaps even further into the future.

Therefore, the overarching question of this book is as follows: Is it possible to plan, learn and train for something that we do not know what is or is coming?

It is extremely difficult to formulate a definition of the concept of the unforeseen that can encompass the above examples and other instances of the unforeseen. Nor are we looking for one. We believe it is appropriate to operate with a definition that is general and minimal, and that is roughly worded as follows (a more nuanced definition of the unforeseen is provided below and in Chapter 5):

> The unforeseen denotes something that occurs relatively unexpectedly and with relatively low probability or predictability for those who experience it and must handle it.

Educational Theory of the Unforeseen introduces new pedagogical thinking to be prepared for the unforeseen to prevent damage and destruction. In other contexts, the unforeseen can be an opportunity to utilize the productive moment for learning. A pedagogy for the unforeseen therefore has two goals, depending on the situation. Firstly, the goal is to use unforeseen moments that arise in pedagogical situations and turn them into opportunities for knowledge and learning. Secondly, the goal is to develop and constantly improve competence that makes it possible to prevent or block the materialization of the unforeseen. These goals are completely different. While the first goal is about seizing and almost eliciting the unforeseen, the second goal aims to prevent the unforeseen from materializing. To achieve this, traditional views of knowledge, didactic models and experiential learning are challenged. Unforeseen events may also be caused by natural forces, or be linked to technological or human failure. The book should therefore be relevant to anyone who works with competence in power, crisis and preparedness organizations, as well as students, teachers and researchers in pedagogy and organizational and management subjects.

The school and education sector, the defence sector and the emergency services are challenged by changing threat situations, the growth of extremism and other unforeseen events. Surprising and unimaginable events can be carried out by both groups and individuals. This places new demands on the sectors' views of knowledge and the content and organization of education. However, the fact is that society at large and each individual are affected by this situation. The unforeseen interferes with everyone's everyday life. This can lead to the risk of society becoming more real for many people. In order to further consider these questions, a more thorough analysis and discussion are needed regarding the challenges that arise from traditional pedagogy in the encounter with the unforeseen. This book is an attempt at such a pedagogy.

Preparedness requires considerable resources and extensive planning, not least in connection with instruction, training and exercises. In order for the learning outcome and the effect of preparedness to be as good as possible in terms of handling unforeseen events, insight into the nature and conditions of the unforeseen is needed, along with basic principles for how such instruction can be planned and implemented. At the same time, we are mindful that this book does not become a supporter of the development of a surveillance society. A pedagogy of the unforeseen is instead more about facilitating an awakening and bringing about enlightenment from a state of slumber.

In the book, we focus on basic issues and targeted analyses of strategic pedagogical problem areas that may arise when planning and implementing instruction to approach unforeseen situations. Therefore, this book is primarily a contribution to the pedagogical discourse within the problem area. At the same time, the book is intended to serve as a basis for those developing more concrete handbooks on instruction and training methods in the fields of preparedness and crisis management. Furthermore, such basic issues will also be relevant as a background for the development of strategic plans within schools and education, in general. However, the book does not contain an exhaustive list of pedagogical perspectives in relation to the unforeseen. Rather, the book presents a selection of such perspectives, based on the authors' research work.

Therefore, the goal is for the book to provide a concrete contribution to further research and discussions, where other and new perspectives can also be formed, for the benefit of education and a safer society.

What signifies the concept of the unforeseen (TU)?

In sum, this book offers many angles on what the unforeseen may entail. In our view, the unforeseen is by no means a closed concept. On the contrary, it is relatively open. With this understanding, the acronym TU is used for the unforeseen throughout the book's chapters.

A key question is what the unforeseen and similar concepts are actually intended to cover. Let us therefore introduce some thoughts and questions on this matter. Are there nuanced differences between concepts such as the unforeseen, the random, the unexpected, the unlikely, the unpredictable, the surprising and similar concepts? Secondly, the question arises as to whether any distinctions in such conceptual and expressive content may be of significance for pedagogical theory and didactic processes, such as planning models, concrete selection of materials and choice of teaching/training and evaluation methods. These concepts can further be seen in relation to phenomena such as knowledge, learning, learning outcome, coping, creativity, judgement, formation, interaction and learning measurement. Several studies and experiences related to incident management and the handling of unclear and unforeseen events show that the concept of knowledge should to a greater extent also incorporate knowledge structures such as creativity, improvisation, flair, tacit knowledge and intuition. The use of simulation technology and scenarios in the learning process may be one approach, but also invites challenges. Therewith, management and organizational structures are challenged: What competence is needed and how can it be developed in a network of interacting organizations and operations? Is it the case that some personality traits are better than others in the encounter with the unforeseen?

TU belongs to a family with more or less closely related terms. For example, we have risk, randomness, unpredictability, unreliability, chance, arbitrariness, probability, peripeteia, surprise, the new, the unexpected and the unknown. This family of definitions is both large and nuanced, as illustrated in Iren Moe's linguistically finely meshed overview (Table 1.1) of TU's closest relatives.

Above we defined the unforeseen in a general perspective as we do not wish to limit the term to any particular context or subject, and then have to worry about the term's area of application. It is minimal for the same reason. Definitions that have a minimal quality encompass a wide range of phenomena, while maximal or detailed definitions would necessarily encompass far fewer phenomena. Therefore, we are seeking a basic understanding of the term that does not specify the type of quantities that can be unforeseeable, nor the degree of unforeseeability

Table 1.1 Overview of nuanced differences in expression of the unforeseen (TU) in relation to risks and dangers (modified after Kvernbekk, Torgersen & Moe, 2015, pp. 31–2)

TU-related words	Explanation	Examples	Others' opinion-related use
The unforeseen	A type of rare, sudden event with a visual character that surpasses most people's imagination, causes extensive adverse impacts at the societal level and can be characterized by the occurrence of known or unknown elements in areas that are not expected or in combinations that have never been seen, but with a cause.	The terrorist attack in Oslo on 22 July 2011.	*Any professional company should be prepared for the unforeseen. In a global survey on crisis preparedness, 66 per cent of managers of large enterprises state that they have experienced a crisis.*
The insecure	Lack of control. Something which you cannot control. Information that can confirm/ deny cannot, by virtue of its nature, be obtained. Can be linked to forecasts and trends.	Natural conditions such as weather and wind. Mental health.	*Risk always relates to what can happen in the future and is therefore associated with insecurity. The insecurity relates to whether a certain unwanted event will occur and what the consequences of this event will be.*
The unexpected The surprising	Used in everyday life and can be both positive and negative. Something familiar arose without having been thought of at the time – unpreparedness. Something occurs suddenly, i.e. coterminous with *surprising*.	A moose crossing the road in a safe place.	*Whether it is as a result of natural, unexpected or deliberate events, the risk of loss of life or harm to health, the environment and material assets is always present.*

(Continued)

TU-related words	Explanation	Examples	Others' opinion-related use
The unclear	Something has happened – but it is difficult to describe the situation. Can be associated with chaos. Use of experience and intuition becomes important.	Extensive fire.	*Today's terrorist threat appears to be increasingly fragmented and unclear.*
The unknown	Something of which one has no knowledge; the knowledge exists, but has not been identified. Most often related to the content of a situation; missing factors in a whole.	Criminal offence; unknown perpetrator.	*All employees shall be regularly reminded to remain vigilant with regard to unknown persons, vehicles, abandoned packages and bags, online activity or other abnormal activity.*
The unpredictable	Something tangible, but you do not know when, where, how or if it will manifest against whom or what. Action without a fixed pattern.	Avalanche. War.	*North Korea is a source of concern due to unpredictable behaviour combined with nuclear capability [...]*
The unthinkable	Something that surpasses the individual's belief in possible outcomes of a conceivable situation. The conditions are perceived as absent; everyday concept.	That Sweden declares war on Norway.	*What is unthinkable? Was the attack on Pearl Harbour unthinkable? September 11? If something is unthinkable, then that is precisely what it is.*

TU-related words	Explanation	Examples	Others' opinion-related use
The uncertain	A sort of time-limited waiting period to receive an answer to something, which can be both advantageous and disadvantageous.	Whether Joshua French is released from the Democratic Republic of the Congo.	*It is, e.g., uncertain how a new war against Iraq will affect stability in the Middle East and the strategies of Islamic terrorist networks.*
The unlikely	Something specific that, due to experiences or a lack of reliable information, one does not believe will occur or has occurred. The degree of probability increases with verified and credible information.	The Norwegian Penal Code's requirement of a preponderance of probabilities.	*It is likely that something unlikely will happen, believes former prime minister Kåre Willoch, who seven years ago submitted the recommendation by the Norwegian Government's Committee on Vulnerabilities.*
The random	Something over which you, in principle, do not have control arises, or could have arisen in a situation without it having been considered prior. The influence or absence thereof can be both fortunate and unfortunate for the optimal outcome of the situation.	That an icicle falls right where you stop at a red light.	*Professional security work and good attitudes greatly contribute to reducing the effect of luck and misfortune, and the Commission's opinion is that most of the observations we have made regarding the tragedy on 22 July are not due to coincidence.*

they must have or for whom. The main point is that TU, which is an abstract quantity, is flexible in the sense that it can manifest itself in many different ways and in different contexts.

What characteristics do unforeseen events have (the nature of TU), and is it possible to learn and practice something that is not yet known (pedagogy for TU)? And what kind of didactics, practical pedagogy, does this require? Through our research, we have developed three main principles which are related to TU.

Firstly, the word 'relative' is included in the definition of TU to indicate that the unforeseen occurs in varying degrees. In other words, there are different degrees of unpredictability, for example, in relation to familiarity/unfamiliarity, how suddenly or surprisingly the phenomenon (or events) occur, in relation to danger signals, or whether possibilities are identified or ignored. These are also important characteristics of the nature of TU. A concrete example of the factor 'familiarity' is that the phenomenon of the pandemic in the context of preparedness will have a high degree of familiarity (via previous events), while the virus SARS-CoV-2 itself (which causes Covid-19) will have a low degree of familiarity or high degree of unfamiliarity. This in turn has consequences for the development of the epidemic and its uncertain effects on individuals, emergency response agencies and society, but also on measures during the situation, often in different ways at different countries and levels, including individual, group, organization and cross-sectoral levels. Here, concurrent learning, meaning learning as the situation develops, will be necessary.

Secondly, 'experience' is a central principle related to TU. This means that an unforeseen event has both an objective and subjective dimension. That means that an event can be experienced (relatively) with different degrees of the unforeseen depending on the person, experience, training, place, time, type of event and not least in relation to emotions and mental capacities to process and handle a lot of information as a basis for decisions and management.

Even familiar events, which have been prepared in advance and which personnel have good training in handling, can contain sequences that are new, or experienced by some as surprising and unexpected. Contingency plans, leadership style, available materials, mastering equipment, improvisation, creativity, innovative thinking and flexibility are also central factors, just to name a few. Furthermore, personality and character traits are central factors regarding TU. For example, some people cope with stress better than others, which can come into play when the unexpected occurs. In addition, the degree of risk, risk analyses and the development of barriers and resilience will play a role, both physically and psychologically.

Thirdly, TU is a collective term for several other apparently similar expressions, such as 'unexpected', 'uncertain', 'unpredictable', 'unthinkable', 'unlikely', etc. There are nevertheless nuanced differences in meaning.

What is the unforeseen about?

Normally, learning objectives are absolutely crucial for learning processes and exercises. It is therefore necessary to develop clearly formulated and detailed learning objectives. That is possible to achieve when the educators know what is to be learned, and whenever the conditions are predictable. However, it is not possible to achieve this in relation to unforeseen events. The reason being that one does not really know what is needed in terms of competence.

This is a fundamental and significant problem. An important part of the pedagogy of TU is therefore to find out what kind of competence is required under such conditions, which can then replace traditional learning objectives, and to develop new and more TU-adapted planning models, which in turn can be used to develop appropriate ways of communication and learning during crises, also in connection with risk communication.

TU is about events and situations that occur suddenly and unexpectedly, just before, during and right after something we refer to as TU-0, meaning the exact moment when the event occurs. TU-0 is therefore a time concept which happens immediately and surprisingly. This can be explained through expressions like these: 'I did not see that coming.' 'We were not prepared for this.' 'It came like lightning from a blue sky.' 'It came straight from the sidelines.' Some have also used the expression 'Black swans' about such events (cf. Chapter 2 for an elaboration of that expression). What we do point out here are events that are not supposed to happen or events that are not planned, but nevertheless happen.

Some specific characteristics of unforeseen events can be described thus: the event occurs suddenly, involving a high degree of uncertainty and unfamiliarity, low unpredictability in terms of how the event develops, few (and perhaps blurred) identified danger signals, complex dilemmas when making decisions and few or no identified connections in the available information. Such incidents also often involve dangers for people, material, society and the environment. However, and this is important to clarify, especially in educational contexts, an unforeseen event can also potentially involve something positive, that is, situations that can be used for learning. There may be incidents that occur in the classroom, for example, students who come up with good suggestions or questions, which the teacher has not planned. There may also be situations that occur in the environment or society, which can also be used in terms of teaching. What is important, educationally, is that the teacher makes use of such opportunities, while abandoning the original plan for a while.

Other unforeseen incidents, such as crises, accidents and disasters, big or small, occur unexpectedly and surprisingly, too. However, these incidents lie at the outer limit of what society, the emergency services or we as citizens are prepared or trained for, or where little or nothing goes according to plan. Even the most predictable events can be experienced as unforeseen and challenge practised routines and patterns of action when they first occur, not least where several actors must interact under risk and unpredictability.

This is therefore not about 'looking into a crystal ball' to find answers. Instead, we are proposing the use of highly advanced approaches and theories to be able to develop new insights and understandings about TU, which in turn can be useful for practice in emergency response agencies and others who must contribute during disasters and other unforeseen situations. To achieve this, the development of new concepts, models and methods is needed, in addition to established theory and methodology.

Why is specific theory development and research needed for the field of TU?

Experience reports from previous events and traditional risk analyses, including resilience thinking (resistance towards unwanted events), are used to determine possible events that may occur, based on history and probability. Based on this, barriers and other measures are developed which aim to reduce the likelihood that something similar could happen again. Nevertheless, unforeseen events do occur. And it is these types of events which are the main focus of TU.

Therefore, there is a need for supplementary theory and analysis methods (in addition to classic risk analysis) as a contribution to understand how such events can happen, how they arise and develop along the way, and to prevent such events from happening. This applies to all phases linked to a course of events in connection with (Figure 1.1):

(1) assessment and foresight of threats or other danger or positive signals (phase 1),
(2) in the encounter phase (phase 2) and
(3) during the stabilization phase or the recovery or learning phase (phase 3).

The didactic Bow-tie model (Figure 1.1) shows that a teacher, or also the students, will be able to experience unforeseen events, both dangerous and positive. The dangerous ones must of course be handled along the way. The positive events should be grasped and utilized for learning when they occur and are experienced in the exact moment when the event occurs, that is, TU-0. During an unforeseen event, there will always be uncertainty. Therefore, improvisation, concurrent learning, trust and interaction will be crucial to succeed in the situation, or to achieve 'good' learning and possible foresight of new events (Torgersen, 2018; Herberg, 2022).

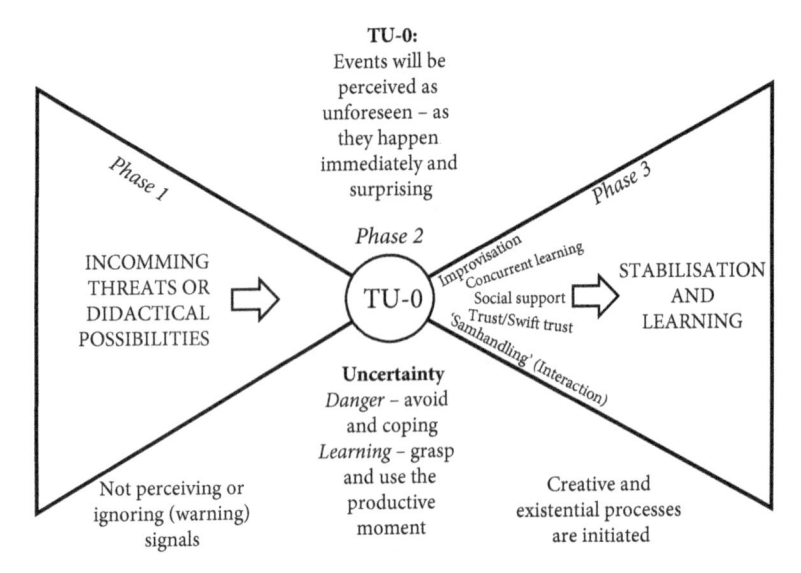

```
                    TU-0:
               Events will be
               perceived as
              unforeseen – as
               they happen
             immediately and
 Phase 1       surprising          Phase 3
                  Phase 2
                         Improvisation
 INCOMMING              Concurrent learning      STABILISATION
 THREATS OR    ⇨  TU-0  Social support    ⇨      AND
 DIDACTICAL              Trust/Swift trust       LEARNING
 POSSIBILITIES          'Samhandling' (Interaction)
                  Uncertainty
                  Danger – avoid
                   and coping
                  Learning – grasp
 Not perceiving or  and use the      Creative and
 ignoring (warning)  productive      existential processes
     signals          moment        are initiated
```

Figure 1.1 Didactic Bow-tie model. The model forms an important basis in the Educational Theory of the Unforeseen. It expresses learning opportunities in all phases of the uncertain, by exploiting the uniqueness of the nature of unforeseen, in a didactic context.

Theory and model development within TU is a contribution to this. The focus will be on investigating the nature of unforeseen incidents, and developing knowledge about nuanced processes linked to the importance of human abilities, management, organizational factors and interaction under uncertainty, dilemmas and unpredictable conditions. Education, training and exercises are essential. To achieve this, new educational models and knowledge principles are needed which are adapted to the nature of the unforeseen.

What are the research focus and the research goals?

Research is being carried out both on the nature of the unforeseen and on what kind of competence is needed to handling unforeseen events, including interaction competence – which turns out to be a decisive competence in many incidents. Therefore, research on the unforeseen and interaction under risk are often linked together.

Research in and on TU is about trying and identifying reality, be it small and large details, that can help us to understand and handle what occurs surprisingly and that can be experienced with a high degree of uncertainty and 'unfamiliarity'. This is also important in light of education, both in relation to preparing children and young people for a world which is characterized by all kinds of uncertainty and aslo preparing them for the great opportunities that can be found in the unforeseen. In principle, everyone has the same ability to use the uncertainty for something positive, as long as this does not involve threats or dangers.

The purpose of the research also has a clear practical and educational aim. The goal is for the research findings and results to be put to use and to have concrete significance as to how unforeseen events can be handled and resolved in the best appropriate manner. That is why TU research is often referred to as being operational, where research findings should be able to be translated into practical action, both in school and in society.

The research objectives are therefore mainly about finding what competence is needed to become better at preventing, utilizing and handling unforeseen events, and how this competence can be developed by way of education – often during the situation, and with uncertain and unclear information. It is a question of both competence in a broad perspective which can apply in all contexts and specific competence which is directly adapted to you, your organization and situation that applies to your reality, workplace, procedures and daily tasks. The overall goal is for the good of individuals, organization and not least for the good of society. To achieve this, one must think both traditionally and innovatively, with regard to theories, models and methods. Cross-disciplinary thinking and approach is necessary.

Danger signals and prevention

All incidents involve some form of escalation, even if this is not identified or taken into account. Training to identify signs or danger signals of escalations, risk scenarios and unforeseen events can be crucial to *coping* with such situations. More general preventive and awareness-raising measures, both in the school and education systems, as well as in society at large, are also essential. Digital social media is also located in this problem area. How should we reflect on and adapt knowledge development for a new reality? What consequences does this have for political formation, judgement, critical thinking, the concept of democracy and, not least, the content of schools in the future? In other words: educators, politicians and other professions – and, not least, the individual citizen – have an important and innovative job to do in this regard.

Time and the unforeseen

Despite thorough preparedness, rehearsed procedures and reaction patterns for all imaginable events, the unforeseen is about situations where what should not occur, nevertheless occurs. The unforeseen is far removed from the calculated symmetry of theory and prediction. Therefore, it is not simply a matter of initiating a programme or performing a calculation to anticipate the unforeseen. This has to do with the fact that any situation that includes the unforeseen goes far beyond the boundaries of rules, programmes, predictions and that which is evidence-based. What happens next will not be a copy of the preceding event. This challenges the principle of experiential learning. Traditional exercises, courses and study programmes can be planned in a classical didactic manner, but as soon as the unforeseen is added as a condition, ordinary didactic models and theories will be insufficient, as such models do not incorporate the nature of the unforeseen. On the contrary, they presuppose a sequence of events that is characterized by linearity, causality and predictability. This applies to both the Continental European pedagogical didactic theory and the Anglo-American curriculum tradition.

The unpredictability and possibilities of the school lesson

Problems and challenges associated with the unforeseen are also present in situations that are not as dangerous or serious, but which are nevertheless characterized by surprises and unplanned occurrences. This may, for example, apply to teachers and their pedagogical planning in schools, where progression in the classroom does not occur linearly according to plan, but is instead characterized by unforeseen and surprising situations during the lesson. Here, the pedagogical principles for the unforeseen can also provide new opportunities, for example, in the relationship between planning, spontaneity and improvisation: Is it possible to adapt the instruction so that unforeseen situations in the classroom can be used as productive moments? Should or can such moments be planned?

What about the school and threat situations in society? Must we become accustomed to living in the danger zone with a certain degree of fear of unforeseen events? Can we be safe without having to relate to such fear? Should students be taught to cope with fear and unforeseen events? If so, what should the role of schools and educational institutions be in such a context? What significance does such an approach have for class management and working methods in schools? Can the teacher accommodate a certain degree of risk in their instruction, with respect to uncertainty, in regard to goal attainment, and by working methods that can challenge students in various ways, including by ensuring that they are trained to improvise and seize spontaneous situations for learning? Such an approach could have an impact on teacher education and how students are prepared for the teaching profession. But where do we draw the line with respect to fear? How should schools, working life and society in general relate to such issues?

These questions concern not only the school's mission and content to prepare students for a future society and working life but also preparation and knowledge-building for the encounter with unforeseen events later in life. Should the unforeseen be part of the principle of lifelong learning? Societal developments may therefore demand the examination of the pedagogy that is applied both in schools and other training and education systems. Perhaps new pedagogical structures should also be developed? Several of the chapters in this book delve into these questions with the aid of various pedagogical perspectives and also suggest some paths that can be taken to address the challenges.

We believe that a new pedagogy is needed, that is, a pedagogy that takes the unforeseen into account. This book suggests some of the approaches that such a pedagogy might encompass, however, without providing absolute answers. Providing specific answers would probably be counterproductive, especially in light of the nature of the unforeseen.

Two main didactic perspectives on TU

In this book, several different nuances on instruction are discussed in the light of TU. We do not wish to categorize these nuances into groups. However, as indicated by the above-mentioned approaches, two main perspectives stand out. One perspective focuses on planning instruction and training that aims to develop the competence to anticipate or prevent unforeseen events, and to cope with such situations along the way, should unforeseen events occur.

The other perspective emphasizes the spontaneous utilization of harmless unforeseen situations that arise in the moment, for example, in a teaching situation, to become productive moments. Utilizing this opportunity for learning and development among teachers and students during such situations could also contribute to students' formation and ability to cope with various forms of unforeseen events later in life, including unwanted events, which are mainly emphasized in the first approach. In this sense, there is a relationship between the two goals for pedagogy for the unforeseen.

Challenging traditional models

The question is how such learning can be facilitated, which basic pedagogical perspectives and which didactic formation and design models can and should form the basis for the development of competence to cope with the unforeseen. Can traditional models be applied? A deeper pedagogical analysis in this regard and a possible revision of didactic design models require an awareness of the theoretical boundaries between the foreseen and the unforeseen, as well as related terms such as *the unexpected, the unknown, the unpredictable* and *the uncertain*. Typical didactic models for planning of teaching and instruction are challenged when placed in the framework of TU, primarily because the learning objective for the unforeseen is unknown.

At the same time, models for management by objectives for enterprises and actions will be challenged by the unforeseen, where too many and overly theoretical objectives that are designed in an enterprise may result in neither practice nor experience being given sufficient space. All in all, this may generate hidden paths and space for unwanted and dangerous actions. Excessively detailed goal maps may, in other words, obscure reality and prevent the direct and immediate detection of danger signals, thereby preventing measures that could anticipate the unforeseen. Educational theory for the unforeseen is therefore a scientific means, in order to grasp the nuances of these challenges, and transform details and connections in what is identified, and transform this into didactic opportunities in upbringing, kindergarten, school, education and lifelong learning.

New didactic models and teaching principles

Thus, is it possible to create didactic plans, prepare, learn and train for something that we do not know what is or is coming? This question requires us to take into consideration the temporal aspect. TU involves anticipation, the here and now and subsequent occurrences. Thus, TU relates to reality, at all times. While theories and models can provide us with an overview of the phenomenon of TU per se, and what can and should be done in a pedagogical context, such abstraction and aggregation of reality, which theories and models involve, may also contribute to obscuring reality. Therefore, we must exercise caution. The British sociologist Basil Bernstein touched on this dilemma by suggesting that reality will always be one step ahead of theories, and that complexity and concretization can bring theories close to reality, but can also increase the possibility that they may be confused with reality, which goes deeper, further ahead in time and can never be fully reached by the theories (Bernstein & Saloman, 1999).

There is much to suggest that the unforeseen follows a different aspect of time, or rather other aspects of time, than the linear and homogeneous view of time of classical didactics. One of the time aspects of the unforeseen implies that time is always *arriving*. It has never fully arrived and thus consists of the incommensurable or incalculable element. We are therefore left with a concept of the future that is not given in advance, in contrast to the linear perspective of time, where the future lies ahead of us and waits with a content that has been conceived in advance, similar to how we think when looking at a clock or a calendar. Thus, it is likely that the anthroposophical hermeneutic pedagogy, critical didactics and, in a sense, traditional views on pedagogy and didactics, due to their strong normative influences, may lead to an immunization of the unexpected, the unknown, the uncontrolled and surprising, all of which characterize the unforeseen. Because of its enigmatic basis, the unforeseen rebels against the frameworks and postulates of theory, and therefore cannot be directly derived from traditional theory or normative and causal principles. Theory and experience may perhaps go some way, but will never be able to fully grasp or understand the unforeseen. This is due to the aporia and enigmatic basis of the unforeseen, which corresponds to an unpredictability that must always be taken into account.

One way to take the unforeseen into account in teaching and instruction contexts is to proceed indirectly, for example, through questions, metaphors, symbols, allusions and silence, where the recipient is given choices and avenues for the existence of more than one way to receive and process the communication. Thus, the indirect form of teaching and instruction will almost force the recipient to avoid placing too much trust in the influence and decisions of others. It is far less complicated to teach and provide instruction with the form of didactics governed by linear and homogeneous time. This is because, here, time progresses in a continuous direction, towards a concrete goal. Although this goal is far from entirely predictable, it is much less unforeseen compared to the heterogeneous time aspect. This means that the educator can to a greater extent designate, more or less directly, what the recipient should do and how it should be done.

Sociopolitical background and current affairs

In practice, this book can serve as a concrete contribution to the development of knowledge that politicians working on education and others have requested in a number of strategic plans and reports, based on the experiences from recent years' serious incidents, terrorist threats and the growth of extremism. Examples include the *Annual Threat Assessment of the U.S. Intelligence Community*. Other countries have similar documents for assessments of threats and security, namely, documents that request greater competence and training on complex and surprising events. The Norwegian Ministry of Education and Research has conducted studies on how Norwegian schools shall be able to cover the competencies students will need in future societal and working life. Currently, there is very little focus on education to cope with risks in society, and even less on how unforeseen events in the classroom can be seized and utilized for learning purposes.

Target audience and examples

At the time of writing, there is no other book on the market addressing the unforeseen in the light of pedagogy and pedagogical research. The target audience for this book is therefore broad, as the message is important for many government agencies, programmes of study and actors in society. However, the book is primarily aimed at higher education in the field of pedagogy and other social science studies. At the same time, the book is also highly relevant for individuals in the defence sector, the police, emergency organizations, the energy and transport sector as well as for the health authorities, managers and politicians. All of these actors have a continuous and strategic focus on improving programmes of study, competence management and other competence-enhancing measures in step with societal developments and new challenges. In this regard, the book can make a good contribution. However, it has also challenged us. It is not possible to design the message in each individual chapter using examples and thematic topicality that are directly related to all members of the target audiences simultaneously.

Towards a definition of educational theory of the unforeseen (EdTU)

Much of the foundation for the book derives from our many years of research. This ensures subject matter precision and reliability, by way of, among other things, examples and our experiences from schools and education. Furthermore, we recognize that the expression of the unforeseen may have different meanings in different organizations, and thus also have different consequences for the pedagogy practised in each organization. At the same time, there may also be certain similarities. We have therefore attempted to make each chapter as relevant as possible for the above-mentioned target audience, where all readers can recognize themselves, and thereby transfer the experiences to their own organization. All in all, we define Educational Theory of the Unforeseen (EdTU) thus:

> Educational theory for the unforeseen (EdTU) is a scientifically based discipline, founded on educational theory and practice, and aiming to develop specific concepts, models and methods, in order to identify, grasp, articulate and express the nuances in the nature of the unforeseen, and furthermore transform this into didactic opportunities and advantages in contexts of upbringing, kindergarten, school, education and lifelong learning.

2

A Brief History of Pedagogy of the Unforeseen

Black swans

In this way, the idea of 'the unforeseen' (TU) is said to be rooted in the term or metaphor 'black swans'. The concept of 'black swans' originally came from the philosophy of science, and it was famously used by Karl Popper (1902–94) and David Hume (1711–76). Philosophers of science used this concept to illustrate logical conclusions from single observations to general principles and general claims.

One example of such conclusions and their limitations in research (and in connection with falsification) was Popper's example of experience with white swans. In Australia, only white swans were observed until 1697. Black swans were therefore considered improbable, if not impossible, because no one had seen them. The logical conclusion was therefore: all swans are white. However, despite all previous evidence and observations, a black swan was suddenly and surprisingly observed in Australia. A new conclusion was then necessary. All swans are not white.

Thus, the term 'black swans' became associated with phenomena that today are considered unpredictable, improbable and unexpected, but still with a certain probability of their existence and relationship to our lives and the world we live in. This is something few people are aware of, which makes it easy to ignore. There are many academic approaches to this topic, but here are a few.

Black swans in finance

The Lebanese American finance analyst and statistician Nassim Nicholas Taleb (1960–) linked the concept of black swans to the study of deviant, unexpected and unforeseen events in connection with risk and risk analyses, particularly related to economics and financial crises. He explained this in his book *The Black Swan: The Impact of the Highly Improbable* (2007). Unforeseen events may trigger financial crises, such as the one in 2008, but the reasons for these events may not be understood until later, or when they are referred to as 'black swans'.

Multidisciplinary approach

Around the same time, an Australian research group with the Australian National University in Canberra developed a somewhat broader theoretical approach to unforeseen events, uncertainty and preparedness related to more multidisciplinary areas and professions, for example, in the areas of health, pandemics, politics, economics, climate and various events occurring in society. This research was reported in the book *Uncertainty and Risk – Multidisciplinary Perspectives* (2008).

About predictions – superforecasting versus the theory of forecasting

Subsequently, many have attempted to continue to interpret and perhaps overinterpret this perspective for the purpose of creating simple models to *predict* events, for instance, in areas of economics and management. One example is stated in the book *Superforecasting – the Art and Science of Prediction* by Phillip Tetlock and Dan Gardner (2015).

In TU research, the primary goal is not to predict but rather to find solutions that can help manage unforeseen events in the best possible way *when* they occur. Naturally, this also involves attempts to find new ways to notice signs of danger from a preventive preparedness perspective. When studying TU, one approach to predict incidents and events would be an awareness of different scientific problems. This type of critical approach can be found in the book *Predicting the Future. An Introduction to the Theory of Forecasting* (1998) by the German-American philosopher Nicholas Rescher (1928–).

Organizational research

The significance of unpredictability related to conditions for organizational development and change processes has in later years also been addressed in light of organizational theory. The American organizational theorist Karl Edward Weick (1936–) could be said to be a representative of this. In his book *Managing the Unexpected: Sustained Performance in a Complex World* (2015), he and anaesthesiology professor Kathleen Sutcliffe (1950–) focus on important organizational preparedness measures to build resilient organizations that can manage uncertainty and sudden, unexpected events. This inspiration is obtained partly from HRO systems (High Reliability Organizations) in the health and transportation sector.

Organizational learning

With respect to organizational learning and knowledge development under unforeseen conditions in organizational change processes, the Japanese organizational theorist Ikujiro Nonaka (1935–) developed several analysis models (including SECI, with the knowledge dimensions of Socialization, Externalization, Combination and Internationalization) related to the Japanese concept of 'Ba', which can be translated as interactive processes during risk and unforeseen conditions (see also Torgersen, 2018, pp. 534–56).

However, the primary focus of organizational theory research is on the organizational level, with less focus on the individual and group levels in terms of learning content and competence for managing unforeseen events.

Traditional risk research

In traditional risk research, with focus on calculated risk analyses related to preparedness, security and resilience, the primary goal is to identify all things that could potentially go wrong, which are organized and sorted into different groups or systems *prior to* any events, so that barriers can be built to prevent unwanted incidents before they occur. This research is largely based on experiences from previous incidents, as well as the frequency of such incidents. This can tell us something about the probability that they will reoccur and thus help determine where efforts should be made to build barriers and resistance, to prevent them from happening again (cf. Saeverot, 2022a).

Resilience research

In the last twenty years, the concept of resilience has gained a stronger foothold in risk research. The term 'resilience' originally emerged in the fields of psychology, medicine, biology and ecology. This term applies to the processes that adapt to or counteract an imbalance that occurs suddenly and unexpectedly, and that steers a system or processes in an undesired direction as compared to the desired and established starting point. The goal is for the system to restore its balance.

These processes are initiated as part of the inherent characteristics of human beings or nature – also in connection with climate change and sustainability. However, such processes will vary in power and efficiency.

For instance, some people are able to manage long-term stress, uncertainty and pain better than others, and with fewer long-term effects, such as post-traumatic stress disorder. In the field of psychology, this is viewed as the individual's inherent robustness and flexibility, or resilience. This is often linked to personal qualities and characteristics such as personality traits.

Resilience in organizations

This perspective was eventually broadened to apply to organizations and their resilience or their capacity to adapt to sudden and unwanted impacts, or to incidents occurring within the organization or society as a whole. Here, resilience is linked to several parts of the system related to the organization, which combined can form a collective resilience, for instance, in the relationship between humans, technology and organizations (the MTO perspective).

The Israeli technology professor Yossi (Yosef) Sheffi with the Massachusetts Institute of Technology (MIT) was part of the group that introduced the link between the perspective of resilience and the ability of organizations to weather unwanted incidents. He did this first in the book *The Resilient Enterprise: Overcoming Vulnerability for Competitive Advantage* (2005) and later in the book *The Power of Resilience: How the Best Companies Manage the Unexpected* (2017).

Definitions of resilience

The Danish psychology professor Erik Hollnagel is also a key contributor to the MTO perspective and the development of the concept of resilience, for example, in the nuclear power industry, through his book *Resilience Engineering: Concepts and Precepts* (2006). He also refers to changes in the definition of resilience in recent years, where the focus on threats and 'the unexpected' as a phenomenon associated with the concept has increased. This is apparent in the development of the following definitions of resilience.

In his first book (*Resilience Engineering: Concepts and Precepts*, 2006), Hollnagel (2016) defined the essence of resilience as the intrinsic ability of an organization (system) to maintain or regain a dynamically stable state, which allows it to continue operations after a major mishap and/or in the presence of a continuous stress. In his fourth book (*Resilience Engineering in Practice*, 2010) Hollnagel (2016) adjusted his prior definition and viewed it as the intrinsic ability of a system to adjust its functioning prior to, during or following changes and disturbances, so that it can sustain required operations under both expected and unexpected conditions. Hollnagel (2016) even proposed a further development as he described a resilient system as something that can adjust its functioning prior to, during or following events (changes, disturbances and opportunities), and thereby sustain required operations under both expected and unexpected conditions.

Nemeth and Hollnagel (2014) have a stronger focus on human and social aspects as an important source of resilience to unwanted incidents, as well as environmental and sustainability aspects. Here, the concept of societal resilience is also used.

Parallel to this was the rise of popular science approaches, where the focus was on both individual characteristics and organizational factors in light of the concept of resilience. This is apparent in American journalist Amanda Ripley's book *The Unthinkable: Who Survives When Disaster Strikes* (2009).

The Norwegian technology and statistics professor Marvin Rausand has a more technology-oriented approach to resilience, which also has an MTO structure. This is described in his 2014 book *Reliability of Safety-Critical Systems: Theory and Applications*.

System versus knowledge structures in resilience research

Although the concept of resilience in recent years has also encompassed and emphasized social aspects such as interactions and learning from an MTO perspective, the approach is still at a general and aggregate level when viewed in relation to actual knowledge structures which are to be present in learning and competence-oriented development processes for achieving such social-oriented resilience in the system dynamics perspective of different levels in an organization. With different levels we mean either at the individual, group or cross-sectoral level.

In other words, resilience research does not go further down into the concepts of knowledge or other hierarchies of skills. They end up at the overall level of concepts, such as 'good cooperation skills', 'facilitating joint understanding of situations' or the importance of 'trust'. 'Deeper' or more nuanced learning concepts such as 'ability to accept little coherence in information, as a basis for cooperation', 'ability for memory in the present to collect information as a basis for common understanding of the situation' or 'spontaneous trust' are ignored and therefore not developed. However, such 'deeper' forms of learning are important to use when developing actual learning processes, formulating competence targets and developing concrete training and learning plans when one is faced with the unforeseen.

Fundamentally, there is a technical, system-oriented and general knowledge and learning perspective, where it is largely the system itself and particularly the technical installations and alarm systems which together comprise barriers and resilience. This will largely work, of course, and in many cases it might be enough. However, to achieve concrete insight, and to identify and develop actual human knowledge structures that should form the basis of a concrete competence framework that can manage unforeseen events, we need a more in-depth and nuanced study of the phenomenon 'the unforeseen', and thus identify and express specific knowledge requirements and learning processes to manage such events.

Learning, training and knowledge structures

This applies not least to transitional phases between identified knowledge, strategic competence development plans, and specific learning and training plans. It would then involve research in order to identify and articulate the content of the knowledge itself at a more nuanced and detailed level. For instance, it would not be sufficient to add 'interaction' as an important factor in a model for managing unforeseen events. The actual, concrete underlying relational factors or knowledge structures that such interactions must contain and be learnt must be identified in order to achieve the desired effect in practice. This may, for instance, include relational factors such as trust, spontaneous trust, learning along the way, involvement, intuition, and the equal and mutual sharing of information during the situation. There may also be different sets of underlying knowledge factors for interactions, regardless of whether the situation to be managed entails risks or whether everything will be happening under safe and predictable conditions. In addition, different underlying knowledge structures may be required, depending on certain phases related to an event. Thus, no form of 'interaction' would have the same content or require the same underlying relational factors during all phases.

Mental skills and capacities – such as the limited processing capacity of short-term memory, learning styles, learning perspectives and didactic education perspectives, which address fundamental ideas about how learning can best take place, especially if the learning content is complex and nuanced – are also part of the efforts to understand which knowledge structures are needed to manage unforeseen events.

From knowledge to plans – curriculum theory

Identified knowledge (cognitive skills, attitudes and emotions) must furthermore be articulated in a comprehensive manner and converted to learning goals, which would be written down in an organization's curriculum and training plans. These would be converted to a concrete and feasible learning content, where it would be necessary to determine the correct progression, select suitable instructional or training methods and scenarios, choose adapted materials and time resources, develop instructor and teacher competence, and find the appropriate evaluation methods to help us know when learning has taken place. These are key factors addressed in curriculum theory and didactics in the field of pedagogical science. This type of insight has been investigated and addressed to a lesser extent in resilience research. It is in these areas that research on the unforeseen, particularly in light of pedagogical science, can contribute to or supplement traditional risk and resilience research.

Resilience versus TU research

In short, traditional research on risk and resilience has been system-oriented with the use of aggregated (overarching) concepts of competence, while TU research focuses to a greater extent on the phenomenon of 'the unforeseen', as well as particular or detail-oriented aspects of competence for managing unforeseen events. Thus, these two approaches complement each other – and together, they constitute a combined force in the attempt to solve the riddle of 'the unforeseen'.

The didactic problem

Such competence enhancements don't just happen on their own. This is a didactic issue. In essence, didactics means the teaching of leading, planning, implementing and evaluating learning processes. Therefore, this involves facilitating learning and competence development for the purpose of managing unforeseen events as well as possible. For a closer look at these questions, we must draw upon a science that specifically addresses this type of problem, and that have methods for this – namely, pedagogical science. This is the scientific foundation for the pedagogy of the unforeseen.

Experiential learning and TU

As mentioned, much of the research on risk has been based on experiential learning, that is, learning generated from previous events, and the attempt to build barriers to prevent such events from reoccurring. However, history does not always repeat itself in the same way, and new conditions may come into play. A situation may also present itself differently than before, which may not have been taken into consideration in advance. Thus, unwanted incidents will still occur. They are part of our reality and lives, and they can happen suddenly and create serious consequences for both life and materials. Things that should not happen may happen anyway.

In other words, several research approaches may be needed to learn more about the nature and aspects of unforeseen events, as well as the type of competence needed to manage such events, especially at the group and individual level. There has been insufficient research in this area.

TU Group

For this reason, we established a research group in 2010 called the TU Group, based at the Norwegian Defence University College. The unforeseen is the TU Group's primary research topic, with an interdisciplinary approach. The TU Group's goal is to learn more about the nature of the unforeseen, as well as the competence needed to manage it, and how this can be developed through learning processes and training scenarios at different organizational levels. To achieve this, the 'reality' must be revealed as well as possible, which entails attempts to identify signs of what actually occurs immediately before, during and immediately after an unforeseen event. Gabriele Bammer, in her book from 2007, expressed this challenge somewhat differently, but with the same meaning: 'Uncertainty is a fact of life' (p. 3).

The TU Group in Norway has particularly worked on pedagogical, psychological and organizational-theoretical questions in light of the unforeseen. It is the theories and models within these disciplines that form the foundation for the problems, methods and analyses. However, unique and specific models for examining TU have also been developed.

TU research examines the learning concept and conditions for learning processes with a more individual-oriented and nuanced approach than that of organizational-oriented resilience and risk research.

TU research in Norway

TU research in Norway actually originated in the discipline of pedagogical science. Based on several foundational research studies and research projects during the period 2003–10, which involved interactions, flexibility and learning in organizations, military pedagogy and the development of pedagogical principles for the Norwegian Armed Forces, as well as new ways of teaching, particularly based on theories of indirect pedagogy, we asked the following question: What does pedagogy have few answers to, and on what has little research been done?

With inspiration obtained from Ronald Barnett's article *Learning for an Unknown Future* (2004), we discussed TU-oriented research strategies and research goals throughout the spring of 2010 and had discussions with several colleagues and students. In the end, we arrived at one question that summed up the core of pedagogical science's blind spots. We asked the following question: Is it possible to plan, learn and train for something that is still unknown?

Pedagogy for the Unforeseen (TUPED)

This was the start of the research project 'Pedagogy for the Unforeseen', financed by the Norwegian Defence University College, which we referred to as TUPED. In the autumn of 2010, the two of us presented our ideas at a large international conference in Auckland, New Zealand, organized by the Philosophy of Education Society of Australasia Inc. Our paper was published in the conference's Proceedings (2011), and it attracted attention from researchers. The title of the paper was 'Bildung, Virtual Terrorism, and Digital Awakening: Towards a Pedagogy for a Discontinuous Future'. This was also the precursor to an article in a special edition about extremism in the Norwegian philosophical journal *Danningens nye ansikt i risikosamfunnet* [*The New Face of Education in the Risk Society*].

Partly inspired by the work of Mark Currie, in his book *The Unexpected. Narrative Temporality and the Philosophy of Surprise* (2013), we gathered several researchers with similar interests and established the TU symposium in 2014 at Akershus Fortress in Oslo, where this research was discussed and further developed.

TU research and publications

Some of the research findings were eventually published in Norwegian in the edited volume *Pedagogikk for det uforutsette* [Pedagogy for the unforeseen, Fagbokforlaget, 2015], which is the first collective introduction to the field of TUPED. Twenty researchers from different fields and disciplines contributed to this volume. An English anthology followed, titled *Interaction: Under Risk – A Step Ahead of the Unforeseen* (Cappelen Damm Akademisk, 2018), which reported twenty-eight studies with thirty-two researchers. Both of these research projects were led by Glenn-Egil Torgersen. The research on TU was later continued at the University of South-Eastern Norway and Western Norway University. This led to a new TU symposium at the House of Literature in Bergen on 1 November 2019, where we gathered twenty international and leading experts in their field based on cutting-edge research, to discuss how education can address existential threats that to a relatively large extent involve unforeseen elements, including significant threats such as climate change, pandemics, decline in global biodiversity, overpopulation, egoism, ideologies, nuclear, biological and chemical warfare, inequality, artificial intelligence, and ignorance and the distortion of truth. This research project was led by Herner Saeverot and resulted in the edited volume *Meeting the*

Challenges of Existential Threats through Educational Innovation. A Proposal for an Expanded Curriculum (Routledge, 2022), which is the first book of its kind to provide an educational and systematic analysis of problems and solutions regarding the most pressing threats facing humankind. With this book, *Educational Theory of the Unforeseen: Educating for an Unpredictable Future*, we are happy to introduce the first international book in the field of EdTU (Educational theory of the unforeseen). The didactic Bow-tie model (Figure 1.1) shows some of EdTU's main generic findings. The model combines the three phases of uncertainty, and which main competences that are important to develop in order to deal with unforeseen events and to grasp moments for good learning, both for teachers, pupils and the society in general. Therefore, this model forms an overall framework for the Educational theory of the Unforeseen (EdTU), and on which more nuanced didactic models and principles are based.

3

Existential Education and the Unforeseen

As far back as the Marshall Plan in 1948, the OECD (The Organisation for Economic Co-operation and Development)[1] has enjoyed relatively strong governance over international education policy. Governance and control were strengthened after the fall of the Berlin Wall in 1989, with the onset of a transnational and hegemonic education policy in which schools and education were linked to economic competitiveness. Thus, schools and education have had the following objective: the individual and nation shall be prepared as best as possible for the international competitive economy (cf. Kristensen, 2017, 2022). With respect to education, we have seen, among other things, that pedagogical concepts have been pushed into the background in favour of 'a number of global-economic concepts such as human capital, human resource, accountability, competitiveness and so on' (Saeverot & Kristensen, 2022, p. 2; our translation). With such global-economic concepts, education policy seeks not least to achieve the OECD's goal of developing pupils' 'twenty-first-century skills' for a new and changing working life. A mindset has developed in schools, education sector and society, 'where quantitative and evidence-based ideals of knowledge are particularly relevant' (Saeverot & Kristensen, 2022; our translation). This can be referred to as the knowledge society. Knowledge and facts are of course good but the education policy developments highlighted here have led us on a one-sided track, which largely ignores important pedagogical focus areas, not least those related to the unforeseen.

---

[1] The original name was the Organisation for European Economic Co-operation (OEEC), which in 1961 changed its name to the Organisation for Economic Co-operation and Development (OECD).

Politicians governing education, from the left to the right, have been singing the same tune for over thirty years. The chorus of this tune is 'more knowledge, more facts and more theory for more money in the treasury'.

The ignorance of the knowledge society

We believe, however, that education should focus its attention on another track – another tune that we have hardly heard before. Here is the first verse or hypothesis. Perhaps more than gaining knowledge, young people today need support in assessing the quality of knowledge. We justify this statement based on the following: children and young people in the twenty-first century have more access to knowledge than anyone else in history, not least through their smartphones. They are inundated with information and knowledge, both inside and outside school. Furthermore, today's youth are swarmed by seductive images and false promises of progress and happiness from influencers, the entertainment industry, social media, the advertising industry and so on. The illusions about happiness and the good life that we are exposed to today are almost overwhelming in Western societies and indeed in a large part of societies worldwide. A pedagogical inference from this is to give young people time and *tools* to reflect on the quality and veracity of these images and all this information and what this might mean for beingness; existence.

Here is the second verse or hypothesis. The knowledge society's one-sided belief in knowledge, facts and reason distrusts passion, emotion and imagination as ways of orienting oneself in the world. With the knowledge society's one-sided pursuit of knowledge, through demands for reason and the greatest possible degree of objectivity, we have developed a blind spot, where such things as subjectivity, intuition and passion have largely been marginalized. However, scientific theorists and philosophers have taught us that it is impossible to be completely objective and uninteresting. We never approach anything with absolute neutrality. Our emotions can serve as a lens through which we can see things we cannot see with reason alone (cf. Aumann, 2019, p. 173).

With these two hypotheses, or verses, we have obtained a draft of a tune that is not solely concerned with facts and knowledge. By focusing on reflection on knowledge, passion, emotions and subjectivity, we are led onto an existential track, where the concept of existential education applies (Saeverot, 2011, 2013). However, in order to more clearly put this into a pedagogical framework, we must first identify the recipient. Who shall the teacher address? While the knowledge society focuses primarily on one type of pupil and one way of communicating knowledge, an existence-based pedagogy relates to at least two types of pupils, who require two different forms of communication (Kierkegaard, 1978, p. 64). Let us therefore take a closer look at both types of pupils and forms of communication.

The unforeseen is not valued in the knowledge economy regime

Thus, our politicians have led schools onto a knowledge economy track and have thereby lulled themselves into a rigid pedagogy that does not take into account that pupils are different. This pedagogy has clear objectives for knowledge attainment and presupposes a pupil who expects and wants to receive predetermined knowledge. Admittedly, a small clause has been added to many of the curricula in the West. It is called differentiation or differentiated instruction, which is intended to ensure that pupils who do not attain their goals immediately can attain them later, but preferably as soon as possible. Since this form of political-economic pedagogy seeks to achieve clear and predetermined goals, pupils' learning will be accelerated so that there is less or no time for being along the way. Thus, pupils have less time to think unfinished thoughts. For example, there is rarely or never time to return to a work, such as rewriting a text or drawing a new drawing. Unpredictability, detours and side roads are not valued in this knowledge economy regime. Instead, results are to be expedited, rather than allowing things mature with the aid of time. The premise is that all pupils and contexts or environments are equal. Thus, the regime misses the fact, which it believes is so important. The fact is that pupils are different and they change from day to day, sometimes from hour to hour.

Relatively frequently, teachers encounter pupils who are distracted, disinterested or somehow oppose the teacher's clear and, perhaps, well-founded pedagogical action. If teachers unilaterally relate to a form of communication that aims to transmit knowledge to the pupils, they fall into a trap that I have observed many times in school: by giving, you take something away. A paradox arises that starts with teachers exercising their mandate given by the curriculum and other frameworks set by politicians. This mandate, which is actually not the only mandate teachers have, is clear that teachers are to transmit knowledge to pupils. The paradox itself arises when teachers deprive pupils of their subjectivity, by providing pupils with certain types of knowledge. Taking while giving occurs because one ignores and disparages the pupils' distinctive reflections, expressions and statements. The mandate to provide pupils with knowledge does not give pupils the opportunity to express their opinions or take a position on what they are told by the teacher.

While the curriculum is primarily written for an ideal pupil who expects and wants to receive the teacher's message and knowledge, in reality, we find many and different types of pupils in the different classrooms throughout the West. A type of pupil who is completely absent from curricula and frameworks are those who will not listen to what the teacher has to say. We also find those pupils who think that they know what the teacher is communicating, but in reality do not. It can also be a matter of information outside of school. For example, we can imagine those who fully believe what an influencer says, but who have not understood the consequences of the meaning of the message when it is brought to life. This is a problem and it does not only apply to pupils. Many of us are satisfied with how we exist in the world, even though we may only exist in a superficial way. Perhaps we are also unwilling to examine ourselves or confront our own self-deception. This problem, which Kierkegaard was concerned with, becomes more serious if we put it into the framework of existential threats that threaten our freedom and the quality of our lives. If, for example, we believe that we know enough about anthropogenic climate change and at the same time live a life that does nothing to respond appropriately to this challenge, then we have a relatively serious problem (Saeverot, 2022a).

Predictable and unpredictable forms of communication

The pedagogical problem, on the other hand, is how to communicate to the different types of pupils? This problem begins with the question 'what do we want to achieve'? The perspective you take is also crucial for the answer you receive to the question. If you take an epistemological perspective, knowledge attainment is the most important, while an existential perspective centres on both knowledge and existence. This has consequences for the selected type of communication.

To take a concrete example, what forms of communication are implicit in the Norwegian curriculum? This curriculum consists of two parts: a curriculum part where the focus is on the training of five basic skills (reading, writing, arithmetic, oral skills and digital skills) and an overarching part where the focus is on morals and ethics. If we look at the curriculum part, which is by far the dominant part of the curriculum, we find an epistemological perspective. As mentioned, if we look at the overarching part, we find a more moral and ethical perspective that will form the foundation of the instruction. Common to both of these is that the pupils will acquire something that is predestined. The curriculum part primarily emphasizes that the pupils are to learn basic skills. The overarching part, on the other hand, points out that the pupils should acquire predetermined values and principles, and, not least, the instruction and training should be based on fundamental values of Christian and humanistic heritage. Therefore, given this predetermination, communication largely takes the form of directness. Let us explain what this means from the perspective of the curriculum's overarching objective: the five basic skills. How do you communicate on the basis of such goals to pupils who are ready to receive it? How do you communicate the rule about commas in the Norwegian-language subject? How do you communicate if the goal is to learn how to use a saw in arts and crafts? How do you communicate if the goal is to add and subtract in mathematics? How do you communicate if you want pupils to learn how many stomachs a cow has in science? Well, you show, explain, instruct, guide, repeat, practice and the like. These are well-known pedagogical measures that can all be said to be direct in form, where the unforeseen, questions or detours have little or no role. Directness often involves telling pupils what to do and how to do it to reach the predetermined goal.

The curriculum therefore has no equivalent for the type of pupil who has a lot of knowledge, but who lacks the ability to put the knowledge into an existential context. When there is dissonance between knowledge and existence in this manner, a different pedagogical form of communication is required than the direct and predictable form of communication indicated by the curriculum. Telling someone directly how they should live is bound to fail. The only thing you then achieve is to turn the recipient against you, and that does not lead to anything good for either the teacher or the pupil. It is therefore more appropriate to use what we refer to with the aid of Kierkegaard (1978) as existential communication, which is more indirect and unpredictable in nature. Herein, there are many forms of communication that can be used where the situation indicates that it is appropriate, such as irony, satire, questions, humour, riddles, hints, metaphors, innuendo, allegories, silence and the like (Saeverot, 2013). It is about communicating in such a manner that the pupils are motivated to want to question themselves, perhaps about circumstances where the way the individual lives now is not appropriate on the basis of, for example, ethical and spiritual values.

It is about finding something that excites curiosity, challenges, inspires and awakens the desire to reflect on what the communicated subject material can mean for your own life. Existential communication aims at the demanding task of living through what you know (Gary, 2007, p. 151).

With the aid of existential communication, you can initiate a movement where stored knowledge becomes action. In this perspective, knowledge should not only be stored in the mind. Knowledge should first and foremost be involved in the way you exist. The teacher's communication must therefore be received as a double reflection (Kierkegaard, 1978). The recipient must reflect twice, in two different ways. The first reflection is a step along the way and is mostly about understanding the words and images that are conveyed. It is only upon the second reflection that one can take the step to become an existing subject. This happens by connecting the words and images to one's own existence.

How do the predictable and the unpredictable work in existential communication?

This dual process assumes two pedagogical goals: a sub-goal and a main goal. While the sub-goal is to get the recipient to reflect on and understand the message in the communication, the main goal is to get the recipient to reflect on what the message means for their existence. The main goal aims at a form of self-reflection that, in one way or another, impacts on the recipient's way of existing in the world. The goal is that what the teacher conveys will be addressed in the life of the recipient. The pupils therefore do not learn from the teacher as one normally does in school. Pupils learn through self-reflection and self-discovery. Rather than ending in learning outcomes and strong performance pressure on the pupils, learning ends in life transformation.

Here, it is essential to understand the basic difference between the sub-goal and the main goal. The sub-goal is in a way objective and falls within the framework of epistemology. It is about understanding the message. The main goal, on the other hand, is existential and subjective, in that it is about converting what is conveyed into one's own. Therefore, the two goals together simultaneously constitute something foreseen and unforeseen. Now, as we have previously mentioned, the terms *foreseen* and *unforeseen* are relative concepts; that is, an event or a situation may appear unforeseen to one person and at the same time foreseen to another (Torgersen, 2015). In this sense, the sub-goal is primarily predictable for the teacher and the pupil, while the main goal is primarily unpredictable for the teacher. It has to do with the teacher losing control at some point in the process (see Biesta, 2014, on the importance of risk in education). If the teacher wants to bring out the subjectivity in the pupils, then the control must at some point be handed over to the pupils. The teacher must let the pupils choose what they want to do with the conveyed subject matter and, not least, allow them to choose how it will become part of their existence. The pedagogy does not necessarily stop here, as pupils may need a co-thinker for their existential choices, someone who can focus attention on their own existence and the obstacles that stand in the way of deeper self-knowledge. Thereby, pedagogy enters an unforeseen space for the teacher, where the teacher must interact with the pupils without having further knowledge of the direction or the goal. It is no longer a question of communicating something, but more so using improvisation (see Chapter 4 for an elaboration on the concept of improvisation), preferably in conjunction with discernment, which makes it possible to respond appropriately to the challenges the pupil is facing.

If the subjective and the unforeseen are not present in the communication, we cannot call it existential communication. If so, we are talking about something else, for example, what can be referred to as behavioural communication – which aims to change pupils' behaviour based on predetermined ideas and motives. Here, only objectivity and predictability are present. We find several such forms of communication in schools, for example, under the auspices of school development programmes addressing bullying and behaviour. Subjectivity and unpredictability are omitted in such ready-made and predictable programmes because it is persons other than the pupils themselves who make the choices. Therefore, such programmes are highly teacher-driven, where the teacher manages and controls what kind of behaviour pupils should acquire. Thus, it is important that everyone should be equal. Pupils should think alike and take responsibility because they are told to take responsibility. We get externally controlled pupils. Existential communication, on the other hand, allows pupils to choose how or whether they want to absorb the communication in their lives at all. This does not mean that you are without responsibility for anyone but yourself. On the contrary: you take responsibility because you want to, not because others say you have to take responsibility. We get self-governing and self-thinking pupils. This is also due to the two perspectives' differing views on knowledge. In the former perspective, it is about knowledge of something (e.g. that a cow has four stomachs). In existential communication, on the other hand, it is about self-knowledge or existential knowledge that is applied in the individual's life.

Unlearning and aesthetic forms of expression in light of the unforeseen

Another pedagogical challenge arises when teaching pupils who absorb knowledge and accept it uncritically, without knowing how that knowledge is put into action. This is an example of ignorance and naivety. Pouring in more information and knowledge will not help this pupil because the problem does not consist in a lack of information and knowledge. Rather, the problem is how theoretical and abstract knowledge can be interpreted and turned into something concrete and fruitful in different life situations.

Let us provide an example of the problem. We imagine a person with a lot of knowledge about climate change. However, the knowledge comes from uncertain sources, such as social media, podcasts and YouTube. The knowledge has not been scientifically verified and is rather fraudulent and false. How can the teacher help such a pupil? Giving the pupil more knowledge on top of the unverified knowledge the pupil possesses could easily create confusion and perhaps worsen the situation. Therefore, it may be more appropriate to first remove the fraudulent and unverified knowledge, so that the learner is ready to receive new knowledge that is more secure and verified. Here we have an example of a process of unlearning (Baldacchino, 2019), which is about assisting pupils who are ignorant, naïve and perhaps even self-deceived, by removing rather than adding. The direct and predictable approach may seem like the most effective way to deal with these types of pupils, but it is not (Fraser & Brown, 2024). Telling pupils that they are wrong or mistaken will likely make them defensive. You are really just giving them an opportunity to justify themselves and their positions. It is therefore not enough to communicate a response to what may be perceived as being mistaken. One must also communicate in such a way that the pupil can detect their mistake without feeling the need to counter. In such situations, an indirect and unpredictable approach is most appropriate, which can get pupils to carry out a reality check without them being defensive (Saeverot, 2022b). For example, aesthetic forms of expression can function as a powerful pedagogical tool so that the pupils can become emotionally engaged and, furthermore, gain new understandings of their ideas, which in turn can change their patterns of existence.

The film *Conspiracy* communicates aesthetically and emotionally and is thereby a good example of the point we are trying to make. Here, we find a dramatized scene from the Wannsee Conference held in Berlin in 1942. In the film, Friedrich Kritzinger (1890–1947) is the only Nazi who opposes the proposal to exterminate all Jews. As a way of warning his fellow party members of what they will face if they carry out such a cruel plan, Kritzinger expresses himself aesthetically by telling a story to Reinhard Heydrich (1904–42), who then retells the story of Adolf Eichmann (1906–62) and Rudolf Lange (1910–45).

> Heydrich: He told me a story about a man he had known all his life, a boyhood friend. This man hated his father. Loved his mother fiercely. His mother was devoted to him, but his father used to beat him, demeaned him, disinherited him. Anyway, this friend grew to manhood and was still in his thirties when the mother died. The mother, who had nurtured and protected him, died. The man stood at her grave as they lowered the coffin and tried to cry, but no tears came.
>
> The man's father lived to a very extended old age and withered away and died when the son was in his fifties. At the father's funeral, much to the son's surprise, he could not control his tears. Wailing, sobbing ….he was apparently inconsolable. Utterly lost. That was the story Kritzinger told me.
>
> Eichmann: I don't understand.
> Heydrich: No?

As Eichmann does not understand the story, Heydrich gives the following explanation, without telling directly what the story is really about:

> Heydrich: The man had been driven his whole life by hatred of his father. When his mother died, that was a loss, but when his father died and the hate had lost its object, the man's life was empty. Over.
> Eichmann: Interesting.
> Heydrich: That was Kritzinger's warning.

Kritzinger's narrative can be seen as a warning and a desperate attempt to unlearn his fellow party members. Indirectly, he said something to the effect of: 'Do not let your lives be filled with so much hate that once the hatred is gone, there is nothing left to live for.' Through an indirect story, Kritzinger created a kind of futuristic scenario and possible consequences that the recipients could imagine.

Art and literature as indirect and unpredictable teaching aids

From history we know that Heydrich and the other Nazis were not persuaded by Kritzinger's story. Indirect communication may not always work as intended. The same goes for direct communication. That said, literature and art occupy a special position when it comes to indirect communication as pedagogical and existential tools. Literature and art at their best do not take full control of their recipients, whether it is the reader or the viewer. This means they do not have a message that conveys some kind of truth to the recipient. Instead, they communicate indirectly and unpredictably, where stories, mysterious relationships, secrecy, magical moments and the like are prominent. Rather than operating with well-founded and reason-based arguments, they speak to our emotions, while feeding imagination and fantasy. In this way, they open the door to the unforeseen and can thus both free us from our cognitive limitations and provoke us to self-reflection and bring forth new insights into our lives (cf. Djikic & Oatley, 2014, p. 498).

We also need reason and knowledge, but often that is not the way to go to create impressions in us – impressions that can make us change our views and course in life. Aesthetic forms of expression, in the form of pictures, stories, films and the like, on the other hand, give rise to feelings that seep into us more than a textbook or a factual report (Fraser & Brown, 2024). For example, we might ask ourselves what is most effective in changing thoughts and attitudes about racism: a reason-based textbook on racism or a film like *Crash* from 2004, which dramatizes prejudice and racism in Los Angeles (Fraser & Brown, 2024). We would almost certainly like to think that the movie *Crash* can grab and move more hearts and minds than a textbook about racism. The reason has to do with the fact that the film's emotional images can be received at a wavelength that is recognizable to many and that we can immerse ourselves more easily in compared to a reason-based textbook (cf. Smith, 2009, p. 58). We humans are not only rational beings but also emotional beings with imagination and fantasy.

TU an new forms of communication

In conclusion, let us emphasize that this is not about dismissing the role of reason and the direct form of communication. The point has been to suggest that schools, teacher education, pedagogy and society have overlooked other important perspectives and forms of communication. In this day and age when we are inundated with knowledge, the primary focus of schools should not be to add more knowledge to pupils. Among other things, we have seen that this easily leads to performance pressure on children and young people and the unfortunate consequences that this entails. In response to this knowledge economy development that has been ongoing non-stop since the Marshall Plan in 1948, we have argued that there should be greater focus on existence, subjectivity, passion, emotion, as well as strengthening pupils' abilities to assess the quality of all the information and knowledge that we all have such easy access to, especially through our smartphones. To achieve this, existential communication must be permitted, where the direct and indirect are not separate categories. Rather, the direct and indirect are part of a continuum, where they intervene in and are derived from each other, much like black and white keys on a piano. That said, the indirect has a stronger impact than the direct when it comes to existence (Saeverot, 2022b). This is because the indirect has better precision; that is, it easily strikes the nerve that causes reflection. On the other hand, indirect communication, like everything else, can be abused by those who use it. Those who use it must therefore have good intentions and know what they are doing, so they do not end up with manipulation and covert indoctrination. Regarding the school's most dominant form of communication, the direct one, it rarely, if ever, strikes the reflection nerve. At best, this form of communication strikes the part in pupils who obey those who give directives. Therefore, direct communication alone is highly teacher-driven, predictable and controlling. It is therefore important that we, and perhaps especially the proponents of knowledge economy pedagogy, bear in mind that teachers with too great a desire to control the pupils through predictability can quickly turn their pupils' free will against them. In that case, nothing fruitful is achieved, on the contrary. In existential communication, on the other hand, all forms of control, predictability and coercion are absent, so that the pupils' free will, which is itself unpredictable, can side with the teacher. We believe that if teachers bring onboard free will, through indirectness and unpredictability, there will be a relatively high possibility that the school can be perceived as meaningful to the majority of pupils, who will be able to voluntarily take responsibility for themselves, for others and for the world.

4

Pedagogical Practice and Improvisation under Unforeseen Circumstances

Introduction

The purpose of this chapter is to examine the potential for improvisation in educational practice. Practical educational approaches can, for example, consist of teaching and supervision, which are part of the pedagogical professional competence, both in teacher training and in the teaching job itself, both in kindergartens, primary and secondary schools and in higher education, as well as training systems in companies and vocational schools. New curricula also specify the importance of teaching and supervision, not least in relation to learning processes with pupils, school development, transition processes between education and profession, as well as peer guidance.

A typical model for pedagogical practice is the so-called didactic triangle (Reier Jensen, 2016, based on Künzli, 1998; Hopmann, 2010). It focuses on relational processes between teacher, student and content. However, this model assumes that the content is relatively clear in advance, and that it has clear learning objectives, or that clarity is built up over time, during the educational practice, and in relation to overall learning objectives and progress. However, not all cases are provided with such conditions. This chapter examines the challenges presented where educational practice takes place if the situation is unclear and unforeseen, and where there are no clear learning objectives. At the same time, we incorporate unpredictable conditions into the relational process between teacher, student and content.

Examples of such unforeseen conditions can be (1) pedagogical processes linked to unwanted incidents, such as conflicts, crises and uncertainty, or also where (2) improvisation is part of the learning process – where pedagogical processes do not have clear learning objectives or where the supervision or the teaching suddenly take a different turn than planned, as a result of the teacher, student or pupil taking advantage of the productive moment which is so to speak invited by the situation or the incident.

The first measure in the event of crises, conflicts and the like, could be in connection with preparedness, or where crises and conflicts have occurred, or are occurring (in the world or locally), and the teaching or supervision becomes an important contribution to children and young people, for example, when it comes to coping with life and mental health.

The second measure will be relevant in the daily work with children and young people, both in kindergarten and school, where improvisation is actually done by everyone, but where the learning potential and nature of improvisation is quite neglected and more or less unexplored. Thus, the content which is linked to improvisation in educational practice will be unclear. Thereafter, the function of pedagogical practice is reduced, seen in relation to the original assumptions and intentions in the didactic triangle.

Improvisation and the unforeseen

Overall, it is necessary to develop this type of model to also apply to pedagogical practice which include the nature of the unforeseen. This chapter examines this in more detail, where the aim is to develop the phenomenon of pedagogical practice to also cover unforeseen incidents and improvisation. The concept of 'Improvisation' is Latin and is composed of Im (=not), Pro (=before) and Viso (=seen), possibly also heard (Montuori, 2003, p. 240). In short, improvisation can be expressed as 'not seen before', and includes meaning about what is not yet known and which appears as unforeseen to those involved in actions related to improvisation. The concepts of improvisation and unforeseen are therefore closely related.

Of particular interest for pedagogy of the unforeseen will be didactic boundary zones between the planned and (transitions to) improvisation (and back to the planned/significance for the plan ahead). Other interests include learning processes related to both improvisation and what importance awareness of these didactic conditions has for the didactic phases, such as management, planning, implementation and evaluation. This chapter will make demarcations in relation to these phases, with an emphasis on planning and implementation.

Problems and questions

In educational research, improvisation has had its main anchoring in an understanding drawn from music pedagogy, especially with experiences drawn from the music genre jazz, as well as drama (Steinsholt & Sommerro, 2006; Sawyer, 2011; Oddane, 2015; Espeland, 2022). Experiences and research on improvisation from music-related approaches and theater activities have been directly transferred to improvisation as a didactic tool in school and educational contexts. That such transfers can be relevant and valid, meaning that they can contribute to strengthening pedagogical practice in relation to aesthetic subjects such as precisely music and drama, can be thought of as both rational and possible.

However, we ask whether such transfer of experience on improvisation from aesthetic subjects is actually also valid in TU didactic contexts, involving school and education. That such improvisation experiences are transferable to other subjects and situations in school and education is nonetheless a core message in both national and international educational research. This is argued by, for example, Steinsholt and Sommerro (2006) and Sawyer (2011), and the same argument appears in several recent articles on improvisation in relation to teacher education (Holdhus et al., 2016).

The basic idea here, which is not touched upon by the aforementioned researchers, is the formal principle of education (German: *Bildung*) which was developed in Germany in the eighteenth century, inter alia, by Friedrich Heinrich Alexander Humboldt. Formal education is, in short, about the fact that knowledge about specific conditions in one subject area can also provide advantages for other subject areas and ways of thinking. For example, we find this in the didactics of language from the 1970s and 1980s, where the claim has long been that 'if you work with grammar, you can practice the ability to think logically, and this work is also transferable to other intellectual activities' (Trygsland, 2017, p. 17; our translation). We find a similar argument in the 1970s' new mathematics and arithmetic with symbols and quantities, where such exercises were supposed to train logic, intelligence and problem solving, to the benefit of all other subjects in school and in everyday life in general.

In pedagogy of the unforeseen, and preparedness research in general, it has long been a basic principle that one can learn from history, or previous events, and in that way be better prepared for forthcoming incidents. However, this is still not clear-cut, as any new incident will never be identical to previous ones. This means that too much focus on learning and exercises on historical incidents, where the outcome has in principle already been laid, may hinder new ways of handling situations, not least with regard to improvisation (Torgersen, Steiro & Saeverot, 2015).

Therefore we ask: How will improvisation work as part of pedagogical practice in a school context? To investigate this further, we also add that the context includes principles relating to the unforeseen.

By way of the French philosopher Jacques Derrida's (1930–2004) ideas of time portrayed as a form of 'hauntology', we examine the concept of improvisation linked to the ability to respond to situations that arise immediately and unexpectedly. In order to concretize and contextualize Derrida's somewhat abstract and philosophical terminology, we analyse and discuss a case from primary school, that is, a pedagogical situation that suddenly appeared outside of planned teaching. Next, we make use of the German educator Otto Friedrich Bollnow's (1903–91) existence-oriented pedagogy, in which we examine the concept of improvisation and whether improvisation from music or other non-didactic areas can be beneficial in general didactic contexts. But first we shall take a look at different definitions of the concept of improvisation.

The concept of improvisation – definitions

As mentioned, there is a close connection between the meaning of the concept of improvisation and handling or experiencing something which is not planned, what we can call the unforeseen. One can thus derive the following formula: Improvisation = The Unforeseen (Montuori, 2003, p. 240). It is important to add, though, that there are many different definitions of the concept of improvisation. Here are some key and selected definitions.

- Improvisation in a teaching context is knowing how to act in the moment, or spontaneously when situations arise in the classroom (that is to say situations which are not planned and may be unusual) (Mason & Spence, 1999, p. 2).
- 'Improvisation is about the ability to solve complex, unforeseen problems with "ingenuity of the moment"' (Oddane, 2015, p. 236; our translation).
- 'Improvisation in its simplest form is reacting spontaneously, from moment to moment – the ability to react actively and consciously in relation to the ever-changing present' (Karlsen, 2006, p. 248; our translation).
- Improvisation is 'a form of reflective practice, where the improviser massages, criticises, restructures and intuitively tests the understanding of something which is experienced here and now […] It is about being present when something happens, an unfolding of abilities and doing at the same time' (Steinsholt & Sommerro, 2006, p. 19; our translation). It is about being spontaneous, in which performance and composition coincide in time (Steinsholt & Sommerro, 2006, p. 19).

- Improvisation is something that occurs here and now in an activity where the participants, in collaboration, create something new and unexpected (outside of a previously given plan or specific expectations) (see, for example, Steinsholt & Sommerro, 2006; Myrstad & Sverdrup, 2009; Sawyer, 2011).
- Disciplined improvisation = a teaching sequence, which is didactically planned; however, with room for improvisation, where time, material and other didactic factors are included in the planning, if unforeseen situations arise (Sawyer, 2011, pp. 14–15). This moment is often referred to as 'moments of contingency' (Black & Wiliam, 2009), or 'Holding Space' and 'Productive moments' and 'TU-0' as well (cf. Torgersen, 2015), all of which have potential to become moments of learning.

Improvisation as 'believing in ghosts' and 'seeing more than we do'

In the above definitions of the concept of improvisation we see that time is a decisive concept when it comes to improvisation, but also with regard to the concept of the unforeseen. We will therefore take a closer look at the concept of time, connected particularly to improvisation and the unforeseen (see also Chapter 7). Time is, however, a very complicated concept. Talking about time as if it were one time is not possible. There are many different types of time, which are often related to one and other, for example, from everyday perception of time to biological time, on to a quantum-mechanical time perspective that is often abstract and theoretical. Although there is more than one time, our everyday life is often governed by so-called clock time, i.e., a mechanistic and chronological time. With the help of a clock we can follow the time and its division into hours, minutes and seconds. Although this is only one way to arrange time, it is in many ways necessary, as we must know when to go work, when the plane leaves or when we should go to the dentist. The watch helps us to keep appointments, and the like.

Yet clock time is not really time. The clock is rather a man-made device that shows 'time', as a way to gain control in everyday life. On the whole, clock time constrains life as everything becomes predictable. This is why educators, in particular those who make use of improvisation, must to some extent free themselves from clock time so as to be able to take advantage of unforeseen situations. If educators were controlled by clock time, and nothing else, the response to situations and incidents would have been predetermined. The future as the unforeseen would have been blocked, by clock time's deterministic division of 'time'. Making space for a different time perspective is thus essential. What kind of time?

In this context we will create an image so that the complexities of time may be more concrete. Thus we relate time to ghosts. For thousands of years humans have been fascinated and intimidated by ghosts. In modern times, and in a literary perspective, we find ghosts in various forms and works, such as William Shakespeare's *Hamlet* (*c.* 1599–1601), Henrik Ibsen's *Ghosts* (1881), August Strindberg's *The Ghost Sonata* (1907) and Jon Fosses' *Aliss at the Fire* (2004). Perhaps the most explicit description of ghost connected to time can be found in the book *Specters of Marx* (1994), written by the French philosopher Jacques Derrida. Therein time is portrayed as a form of 'hauntology'. The logic of hauntology is that time haunts us like a ghost who comes and goes, without us knowing when this might happen. In such a conception of time, let us for the sake of order call it 'ghost time', the 'ghosts' of lost futures haunt the present. Ghosts always return to haunt us, with unrecognizable forms. Expressions such as 'time goes so fast', 'time goes so slowly' and so on are embedded in our language and thinking. This is how language and thought are governed by clock time's deterministic logic. As for ghost time, on the other hand, time does not go forward; rather, time comes to us. Time seizes us, it touches us, often before we are even ready or prepared. Suddenly something unexpected happens in pedagogical practice; for example, a phone rings, without warning. Or think more generally of that time you were scared, totally taken aback, while your body squirmed. Ghost time surprises us.

To be surprised means that we cannot know what is happening in advance. For example, if the artist tells you what his or her artwork is about, or if someone reveals what is happening in a movie, a so-called spoiler, the moment of surprise disappears. The reason being that we have an idea of what to expect. It's as if the future is waiting for us. That is why ghost time does not appear in thoroughly planned and fully controlled education. Such education lacks veils, where more or less everything is obvious, predictable and transparent. One can, so to speak, look into the future and there is nothing to wait for. But then there are also education which is similar to the real world, in which there is room for the present to be haunted by ghosts.

Where do the ghosts come from? Is it the educator who has included the ghosts, or shall we say the futures, in the pedagogical practice in advance? Is the educator the origin of the ghosts' haunting? Sometimes yes and sometimes no. The educator has planned the teaching or supervision and has thus something to do with the creation of ghosts; however, there are also forces at work in pedagogical practice which are not too carefully planned, forces over which the educator has no control. This is how the ghosts can haunt such educators again and again, in ever new shapes. They are created and recreated without the educators being able to point to a specific origin. In the idea of hauntology, the future has no origin. Yet time comes to us, it touches us, and perhaps it gives us a ghostly shock. Such a time is not possible to seize in advance, because it seizes us, and since we have been seized, the past has already appeared. Ghost time is first experienced as a past.

If the future was like a programmed calculation and we could see exactly what would happen, or if we knew when the ghosts would come, we would be able to set the clock by them, but then we would not have anyone or anything to wait for. Another thing. The ghosts that emanate from education which are not too carefully planned are also well protected, as the ghost in *Hamlet* hid by the visor and armour. This in turn means that educators who improvise must relate to the unforeseen as an invisible visibility, as an invisibility-making of an appearance. The same goes for the other senses, for example, the unforeseen as an inaudible audibility. Derrida of *Specters of Marx* argues this point eloquently and persuasively by way of the idea of the power of absence. As such, the book speaks indirectly of a ghostly world which is invisible and well hidden, not because it hides behind something, but because it at times dazzles us. What does this mean for educators who make use of improvisation? They must learn to see what is invisible and hidden (or hear what is inaudible, etc.). By seeing what is invisible, new opportunities for learning can come to us. How may this be possible?

A negative answer to this question, that is, how educators should not improvise, is to engage in a form of 'ghost hunting'. Admittedly, it could have been quite exciting, as we could have acted as 'the ghostbusters' who hunt for ghosts in the movie *Ghostbusters* from 1984, but that is not what *Specters of Marx* proclaims. Hunting has become a fashionable term, and we find it in TV shows and books, and so on. The point being that the hunting or pursuit of something entails a different time logic than hauntology's logic of time. If we take a closer look at the concept of hunting, it is basically about tracing and outsmarting an animal, but it can also be understood as a search for some form of truth (e.g. about a famous person), or something that in a normative way is considered to be good (e.g. a good life). In any case, any educator following a hunting logic would probably overlook the invisible that appears in the visible, because it is the hunter who is tracking something or someone down. We could easily end up with a form of exorcism where 'the ghosts' are driven out and away from the educational situation.

In the framework of hauntology, the logic of hunting is turned upside down. The reason being that we are haunted rather than hunting. It is not the educators who seek or track down; rather, something or someone seeks us, our mind and our body. Does this mean that educators should be passive and wait to be haunted? No. In order to see the invisible in the framework of hauntology, something is required of educators. What? Mainly two things. First, they must, metaphorically speaking, 'believe in ghosts', or believe that there is more between heaven and earth than what they see. 'Believing in ghosts' means having faith that there is more to see than meets the eye. The same principle applies when listening to someone speaking. You hear what they say, but you have to believe that there is more to what they say than what you hear. Those who do not 'believe in ghosts' will most likely never see the invisible, and will therefore not receive new opportunities for learning. Let us explain in more detail what we mean by our metaphorical formulation. The expression 'the first impression is so important' may be correct in many contexts, but in the framework of hauntology it often turns out to be wrong. This is because the first impression, or more precisely our first glance at something, for example, a particular situation in educational practice, is blind to the invisible. The strange thing is that we often see the invisible, but we do not notice it. The invisible does not hide behind anything; it is right 'there'. It is as if the ghosts are rattling with their chains right in front of us. But those who do not believe in ghosts, that the invisible appears in the visible, will not see them. They think they see what is to be seen; however, they can only see what is visible. They do not hear the whisper of the ghosts, the ones that alter, keep renewing and reforming what we innocently call the contemporary.

Secondly, educators need to 'see more than they do'. We admit that this, too, may be perceived as a rather abstract formulation. But what it means is that the educators must see what is invisible and hidden. Those who believe in ghosts will always strive to get past the first glance, so that they can see what the first glance actually sees, but is unable to notice. Getting past our first glance is like indulging in the invisible. It is about evoking the ghosts, the visible invisible and let ourselves be haunted. This too may sound abstract, but it is our belief that many have experienced hauntings, that we have overlooked something, for example, when we watched a movie or read a novel. But then, when we went back, and looked again, we suddenly saw something that we did not see the first time. In such cases, one is often left with this feeling: 'It is so obvious, why did I not see it right away?' The art is thus to notice what Derrida of *Specters of Marx* says indirectly – because it can turn out, and it often does turn out, that an expression, a sentence or a passage from educational situations is conveyed indirectly and thus made invisible (Saeverot, 2022b). At first, it may sound as if pupils or students are saying one thing, when in fact they are saying something completely different. Thus, educators will probably miss the most important thing that is conveyed. To live up to such an art form is easier said than done, but the educators who are able to do so can make the impossible possible; namely, to receive hidden knowledge, and to respond appropriately, as part of an improvisation.

Ghost time and improvisation – a case

How can this abstract and philosophical ghost time be connected to improvisation in relation to pedagogical practice under unforeseen circumstances, and thus appear more concrete for educational matters? To answer the question, we will analyse and discuss a case with a teacher who neither 'believes in ghosts' nor 'sees more than what he sees', as he is faced with a conflict situation involving the unforeseen.

The main characters are two boys in the sixth grade – 'John' and 'Allan'. They play with some pupils in the second grade during recess. The play may appear to be a bit violent from the outside, but everything is under control. Suddenly and unexpectedly, a boy in second grade intervenes. He has not been part of the play. He has seen it from a distance, and breaks in and kicks John in the leg. It may seem that the second grader has misunderstood the play and wants to defend a fellow pupil. He has misunderstood because he has interpreted the play too literally. John gets angry and pushes the second grader, causing him to fall. The boy starts to bleed from his hand. The recess is over and it is time to eat. Inside the classroom, one of the male teachers will bring up the incident with John and Allan.

> Teacher to the two sixth graders: 'Would you like to come with me and have a talk?'
> Allan: 'I'm eating.'
> Teacher: 'What did you say?' (*He asks even though he heard what Allan said. The teacher is obviously annoyed.*)

Allan repeats: 'I'm eating.'
Teacher: (*braces himself*) 'OK, then we'll have a talk after you've eaten!'
Allan: 'I don't want that.'
Teacher: 'You, come here!'
Allan: 'No.'
(*Teacher rushes towards Allan and grabs him by the collar of his jacket and lifts him up from the chair. Allan starts to cry and runs out of the classroom and leaving the school.*)

First, was it justified by the teacher to start with the following question to John and Allan? 'Would you like to come with me and have a talk?' Let us first view it from Allan's perspective. He is an intelligent boy and interprets the teacher's action and inquiry as meaning that he and John had done something wrong. From Allan's perspective, this is the prominent view in the case: He thinks that the second grader who kicked John started it all and is the one to blame. Allan is clear that he and John played nicely with the second graders, before one boy misunderstood the play and kicked John. Here we must remember that play has an indirect and invisible perspective. In play, one pretends, the roles played must not be interpreted literally. This is why play has an indirect element. If the play is interpreted literally, and the invisible in the visible is overlooked, it will be misunderstood. This may be one reason why Allan responds thus: 'I'm eating.' Moreover, he also responds in such a seemingly provocative way to tell the teacher indirectly that he thinks the teacher is prejudiced as he has decided that he and John are guilty in the matter. He is certain that the teacher has decided the question of guilt and that it is no use persuading the teacher otherwise. The teacher, for his part, overlooks Allan's indirect message. He does not see the invisible that appears in the visible as we explained in the previous section about ghost time. This shows that the teacher does not 'believe in ghosts' and that he therefore does not 'see more than what he sees'. The teacher addresses John and Allan based on something foreseen. He has formed an image where a second grader has bled from the hand and that a bigger boy in the sixth grade has caused this.

Thus, the subsequent 'talk' is determined by something foreseen which entails that Allan initially opposes the whole thing. Allan is sure that 'have a talk' means that the teacher will reprimand him based on the foreseen image that the teacher has formed in his mind.

Allan is also intelligent enough to see through a form of freedom which is really a coercion from the teacher. What we mean is thus: even if the teacher asks, 'Would you like to come with me and have a talk?', Allan and John have no choice but to be 'guided' by the teacher. Thus, all possible improvisation is stopped and blocked in the first place, by the teacher. That is because his question is anything but open-ended, it is only a rhetorical move and an indirect way of hiding the coercion in the question – so that the question does not sound as direct and coercive as it actually is. It is a misuse of indirect communication, as the teacher resorts to hidden coercion (Saeverot, 2022b). At the same time, the teacher has done the opposite of what improvisation is about. He has neglected the 'im' (=not), the first part of the concept of improvisation, and has thus 'seen before' instead of 'not seen before', as we emphasized above. This means that the teacher relates to something foreseen, the very opposite of what improvisation is about. It shall also turn out that the assumption that there is hidden coercion in the teacher's question is valid. We see this as the teacher's level of irritation increased, until he resorted to force and violence. Admittedly, the teacher managed to control himself at first, as he replied to Allan like this: 'OK, then we'll have a talk after you've eaten!' He lets Allan finish eating, so he gives Allan something, but there are no signs of improvisation as 'not seen before' because in his response, the teacher reveals that there has never been an option that John and Allan can choose not to have a talk. Thus, his initial question was only a rhetorical device. Allan's assumption is correct and his psychological game works. He manages to provoke the teacher, even if it is first and foremost a signal that he does not want to talk about a play that he thinks a second grader is to blame for ruining.

Let us also not forget that the relationship between a teacher and a pupil is uneven when it comes to several things. The teacher has more experience and power than the pupil, but is not necessarily more intelligent and wiser than the pupil. The teacher has also more authority than the pupil. This is because the teacher is the one who shall teach, educate and guide the pupil. If the pupil contradicts this, or shows disobedience, the teacher can show his or her authority in various ways. The teacher from our case obviously has a view that he has the right to force his pupils to 'have a talk'. When he then feels that his authority is threatened by a pupil, he resorts to force and violence. We have a pupil who does not want to be forced, but shall be forced by the teacher. This is how the trust between the teacher and Allan is broken. This means that Allan cannot trust the teacher, because if he opposes the teacher, the latter will make use of force and violence. A teacher-pupil relationship without trust is worthless. Education requires trust as a foundation of the relationship between teachers and pupils. There is another point that is important in this context. Teachers are obliged to promote a pedagogy that is in the best interests of both individual pupils and groups of pupils. At this point we touch on a fundamental difference between improvisation in music and didactic improvisation. In music, one does not have such an obligation. Here, musicians can simply improvise, based on purely aesthetic aspects, where they are looking for what sounds best in a specific context. Teachers who improvise, on the other hand, have to deal with the unforeseen, while at the same time as they are obliged to safeguard the pupils' rights, legal, ethical and pedagogical (Roberts & Saeverot, 2018). It is obvious that the teacher in our case has neglected all this. He has neither improvised (as 'not seen before') nor taken care of his obligations. Rather, he has done the opposite, in the sense that he has 'seen before' and resorted to the use of force and violence.

The entire situation description shows that unfortunate consequences can occur because certain parties do not 'believe in ghosts' and thus do not 'see more than what they see'. This is how the indirect communication which is at play in this case is overlooked and misunderstood. The second grader who kicked John on the shin misunderstood the indirect elements that were embedded in the play. He did not see the invisible element in the play. The teacher, for his part, was totally blind to Allan's indirect message, where the words 'I'm eating' became a provocation. An important point here is that both teachers and pupils make use of indirect communication all the time. That means that 'ghosts' become part of communication, for example, between teachers and pupils. In other words, language and communication are often full of indirect and invisible messages, signals and other, more obscure things, which one cannot see at first glance. Therefore, one must try to look past one's first glance in order to notice something more, that which is 'not seen before' and which is crucial for didactic improvisation. If teachers do not 'believe in ghosts', they will most likely overlook the invisible that appears in the visible. This can have very unfortunate consequences, as we have seen in the above case. If, on the other hand, teachers are aware that situations and the like can consist of 'ghosts', that is, something that one is not able to see or grasp at first, they can use such situations pedagogically, not least in connection with improvisation under unforeseen circumstances. The reason being that such teachers are not totally certain before they act with their pupils. In other words, such teachers have not 'seen before', and will thus avoid going into situations where they have decided things in advance, without taking the trouble to ask and be open for 'ghosts' at play, that there is something hidden in the visible. At the same time, such teachers relate to the assumption that situations often contain something more than what they initially seem to contain, and such teachers therefore approach this in a more open and questioning manner, with opportunities to improvise and grasp and respond to what is 'not seen before'.

In this case, on the other hand, the pedagogy sort of takes place before the situation itself. This means that the teacher has concluded in advance. Thus, he blocks possible learning moments from the situation with John and Allan. At the same time, the teacher is met with something unexpected and for him a negative perspective, as Allan responds that he does not want to come along to have a talk. From one perspective, one could argue that the teacher is improvising when he says that they can have a talk after the boys have eaten. But, it is a form of improvisation that is equivalent to 'seen before', because his response is set in a predetermined framework, in which he has decided that Allan and John must have a talk. The talk has only been postponed to a later time. Although the teacher blocks the unforeseen in this way, he also controls the future – which will be different and unpredictable in the sense that the teacher's expectations are not fulfilled. From the teacher's perspective, the future comes to him as something not expected and desired.

As pedagogy in classrooms consists of both planning, routines and practical tasks, it also consists of moments, there and then. It is something very short-lived, but from such short moments essential things that are important for learning may occur. It will require a completely different approach to the one we have witnessed. Not least, teachers must be more open. Thus, the teacher in our case should not have spoken to John and Allan while they were eating. Instead of talking to them in front of the whole class, he should have brought up the matter with the two boys alone. He should also show that he is genuinely interested in finding out what happened, and let the boys understand that their version of the incident matters. From there, the teacher could be able to perform what we will refer to as 'spontaneous improvisation', where the teacher allows moments to become the moment that Allan and John have. Spontaneous improvisation is about being able to seize a here-and-now moment, and in that way meet the pupils where they are (place), both here (place) and now (time). In this way, the pedagogy deviates from the planned and becomes spontaneous improvisation, where the teacher listens and looks for more than what he hears and sees – so that he is able to grasp something not previously thought of. What occurs in the present becomes more valuable than what the teacher has thought in advance.

So in such situations, the teacher must put aside the plans and routines of teaching, which follow the chronological order of clock time, and rather direct all attention to that which occur in the moments, which follow the logic of ghost time. Furthermore, the teacher must make assessments in moments, assessments that in the best possible way make sure that the boys can express their perspectives on what happened in the schoolyard. What this means is that the teacher is not looking for something specific, for example, to find a scapegoat. In contrast, the teacher is completely open to what all parties, including himself, can learn from the situation.

Spontaneous improvisation is very complicated, perhaps the most complicated of all pedagogical actions. The reason being that the teacher must be able to seize moments that will never return in the same form. To improvise spontaneously therefore always means starting over. There are no methods or recipes for what to do. The closest 'method' we have is to 'believe in ghosts' and to 'see more than what we see'. And this must be done in every single situation that arises, where spontaneous improvisation is relevant.

Improvisation, risk (*Wagnis*) and failure

So far we have argued that there are aspects of education that make the pedagogical work immediate and unpredictable. This was shown in the case where the teacher wanted to have a talk with Allan and John. To the teacher's surprise, he received a different response than what he had imagined. Thus, the whole situation took an abrupt, unexpected and unfortunate turn. As soon as the unforeseen comes into play in pedagogical practice, an element of risk appears, or what in German is called 'das Wagnis' (Bollnow, 1969). The late German educationist Otto Friedrich Bollnow emphasized that *Wagnis* (which cannot be translated into English) is something more than risk, which we will soon explain in more detail. In short, *Wagnis* is relevant in situations which make room for improvisational responses which are highly uncertain. As a teacher, you must dare to respond improvisationally, even if you cannot be sure that the improvised response you choose to take is good or bad for the pupil. Teachers can therefore risk doing something wrong when they improvise, which can have fatal consequences, primarily for the pupils, but also for the teacher involved. There are thus possibilities for failure.

On a music scene, things are quite different. Here, for example, jazz musicians can make errors while improvising. As such, there is an element of risk here, too, but you cannot talk about failure in the same way as in an educational relationship. Let us explain. Improvisation in a didactic situation involves acting immediately. Teachers must respond immediately to unforeseen moments that arise. Teachers thus face something they are not prepared for. It almost goes without saying that it is very demanding and that one can risk making errors, which can be particularly poignant, shocking and painful for both pupils and teachers, in contrast to what a musician will experience when they improvise (Bollnow, 1969). Of course, a musician can feel failure, but it does not affect anyone else in the same decisive way as it can in an educational relationship. The musician does not have, in contrast to a teacher, 'a deep and binding responsibility', as Bollnow (Bollnow, 1969, p. 152; our translation) puts it.

The Danish phenomenologist and theologian Knud Ejler Løgstrup (2000) is known for an expression in this context which underlines that we have responsibility for the destiny of others, which we hold in our hands. For teachers, this means that they have their pupils' lives and destinies in their hands. Therefore, it may happen that things teachers say and do can have unfortunate consequences. If we imagine the consequences on a scale, we can imagine that the consequences have different degrees, from high to low. On one extreme side of the scale, one can imagine consequences that are hardly noticeable, while on the other extreme, one can imagine that teachers can ruin the lives of their pupils. For example, it has happened, fortunately not often, that pupils have taken their own lives because of teachers' actions.

Now, what is the rationale for using the German concept of *Wagnis* rather than the concept of risk? For sure, there are several concepts and terms which can be used in relation to aspects related to uncertainty and unforeseeability – which are involved in not knowing the future. Bollnow (1969, p. 146) makes use of three different concepts in this regard: risk, attempt and the untranslatable concept of *Wagnis*, all connected to various aspects of education's uncertainty (Bollnow, 1969, p. 146). For example, Bollnow connects the concept of risk to the chances we take when we do not know the outcome of our actions, whether we will gain or lose something. For example, businesspersons will run a risk with their dispositions, because the result of their endeavours is dependent on factors that are difficult to know with certainty in advance (Bollnow, 1969, pp. 151–2). According to Bollnow we also run a risk when we plan to go on holiday. The reason being that we do not know what the weather will be like, thus we do run the risk of having bad weather on our holiday. Nonetheless, we often do take the chance and go anyway (Bollnow, 1969, p. 152). Such types of risk may be found in music and, in fact, in all professions. However, in didactical situations things are quite different. That is why Bollnow makes use of the concept of *Wagnis*, which is a more existential concept than risk. The reason being that *Wagnis*, when it fails, touches a person's inner self and may affect our lives (Bollnow, 1969, p. 152). As for risk, it does not necessarily affect the whole person. That is certainly not the case for *Wagnis*. When *Wagnis* fails, the whole of human existence is at stake.

This can be explained by going back to our case, which involved a teacher and the two students, Allan and John. The teacher never witnessed the actual incident that happened in the schoolyard, but had the incident briefly recounted by some pupils who had been present. The fact that a smaller pupil had been pushed by a larger pupil, resulting in blood, had made a strong impression on the teacher. This perception set off strong emotions in the teacher. He then took all this into the classroom. Here, the teacher expressed quite sternly and firmly, 'Would you like to come with me and have a talk?' It is a question, but as we have discussed, in reality it appeared more like a hidden coercion. The teacher was concerned with the question of who was to blame and had decided in advance on the issue of guilt. This was noticed by Allan, who wanted to defend his right to finish his meal. He therefore said that he would not come along to have a talk. The teacher perceived this as a provocation, which showed in his further 'improvisation', understood as 'seen before'. Thus it all escalated and the teacher finally physically grabbed Allan who ran away from the school, crying.

Then a new element enters this case. Later in the day, the teacher calls Allan's parents on the phone. Here he says that he has done something stupid and that he regrets terribly what he has done. He tells Allan's parents that he takes all the blame for it all. The teacher has had a harrowing experience and he acknowledges a major failure as a result of his wrongdoing. Allan, for his part, never spoke about the situation and we do not know how things have gone with him since. But we can be sure that the incident has probably left an eternal mark on him, and that he, too, has felt the feeling of failure. The reason for this is simple: an adult, one of his closest ones, had first decided that he had done something wrong and then used violence against him. Allan must have felt a tremendous mistrust from his teacher and one can easily imagine that he can hardly trust this teacher, and perhaps he also becomes extra suspicious of other adults with whom he associates, which makes it difficult for him to build up good relationships of trust with adults in the future. However, this is only speculation and is of course dependent on many different factors.

5

Didactic Models for the Unforeseen

A need for new models

In this chapter, we describe some of our research findings in a more practical way to form the basis for didactic models of the unforeseen. More specifically, we introduce two didactic models: Strategic Didactic model for The Unforeseen (SD-TU model) and the Didactic Balance Model (DBM model). The SD-TU model is a more holistic planning model to include unforeseen events in various types of teaching and exercises. This includes many factors that teachers and educators should reflect on in their didactic choices in planning, implementing and evaluating teaching for the unforeseen. The DBM model is linked directly to such reflections regarding didactic choices. In this context, it is necessary to balance between different extremes and possible outcomes, which can be fortunate or unfortunate, either in relation to the purposes of the teaching, or whether spontaneity and improvisation itself should be allowed to control the direction and the outcome of the teaching. The DBM model acts so to speak as a sparring partner in relation to the didactic choices. For both models, the didactic Bow-tie model (Figure 1.1) is a foundation, in order to be able to navigate and orient oneself in terms of different phases of events, etc.

Both models can be used in order to both develop and constantly improve competence to handle unforeseen events, and to utilize unforeseen events for learning. Whilst the SD-TU model can help to provide a systematic overview of important factors in practical teaching planning, the DBM model is a means for reflection in the didactic choices made when using the SD-TU model. That being said, both models can of course be adapted, developed further and used separately.

Concurrently, we believe that every organization should reflect on how they relate to the concept of TU, how they perceive and understand it, and the importance the understanding may have for the enterprise, inter alia, for education in the organization. Before we introduce the didactic models, we will therefore return to the concept of TU to understand the very basis of the models.

The concept of the unforeseen – the Nature of the Unforeseen

We begin by redescribing the short definition of TU from Chapter 1 to provide some more nuances to the definition (Torgersen & Saeverot, 2015, p. 318):

> A relatively unknown event or situation that occurs relatively unexpectedly and surprisingly with relatively little probability or foreseeability for the individual, groups or society that experiences the event and consequences, and must potentially deal with it.

Let us henceforth take a closer look at the content of this definition, as it helps us to grasp and articulate nuances in the unforeseen, which can open up new didactic possibilities.

Relation and continuum

In the definition of TU, we make use of 'relative' as the relational and continuum adjective before 'unknown', 'unexpected' and 'probability'. We have done this to indicate a fictional difference between the foreseen and the unforeseen. It will be those who experience the event and the uniqueness of it who will in practice decide how foreseen or unforeseen the event was. Theoretically, we can also place a continuum between the foreseen and unforeseen within a delimited frame referred to as the total foreseen or total unforeseen. At the outermost limit for the unforeseen, the conditions for 'unfamiliarity', 'unexpectedness' and 'probability' (improbability) must also be the total conditions for those who experience it or for the society or world at large as well. Within these outer points, there will be a continuum of possibilities and levels or tiers. With uncertainty analyses, it is still common to use three tier levels. In this respect, 'probability' is ideally assessed according to three 'tiers', low, medium and high, both in relation to the prediction of possible events and consequences (low, medium, high – severity level of the consequences) should the event occur (Austeng et al., 2005, pp. 57, 88, 127–8). Similarly, the concept of risk can be applied to indicate the probability of something happening (low, medium or high risk) or to indicate the risk of error or failure, or exposure to an accident when managing and implementing measures for the events that occur.

Tiers of unforeseeability are an important point of departure for the possibility to train for unforeseeable events and have been included in our didactic model for this type of education and training.

We also use the expression 'occur' in our definition. The reason being that an event always has an escalation, a process and is long or short in time with signs that are either identified and taken into consideration, which contributes to triggering an alert about the event, or the signs are not identified or taken into consideration. Within the field of emergency management, the expressions 'sudden crisis' and 'looming crisis' are ideally used for events that occur abruptly with a relatively short escalation period or which develop over time before they are uncovered (Lunde, 2014, p. 40). Both types can be perceived as surprising with no given notice, since the warning signs are not detected.

Further, the notification of an event, for example, a fire or accident, can at any time take unexpected twists and turns during the course of the event, in view of what is expected, throughout the entire process from notification of the event until it is under control. As such, the parts of the event and development can also be classified according to various levels of unfamiliarity and unexpectedness during the course of the event, which the actors are not prepared for, both factually (objectively) and in relation to the individual's understanding of the situation (situation awareness). Accordingly, the expression 'unpreparedness' will also be a descriptive term in relation to the unforeseen. In risk management and emergency management, the concept 'unwanted incidents' is also used for all events that may lead to obvious adverse consequences for the enterprise (Lunde, 2014, p. 39).

Degree of TU

Unforeseen events can neither be 'totally unknown' nor 'totally known'. Such events would be in a continuum *between* these fixed extremes, denoted as the 'continuum-field'. An unforeseen event can divided into, for example, five main categories or TU-factors – within a degree of (1) *Relevance* (to the target audience), (2) *Possibility* (of occurrence), (3) *How known* (in advance by the target audience), (4) *Warning signs* (scope/number) and (5) *Warning time* (for given/ identified warning signs and exercises, for example, unannounced exercises).

The degree of the unforeseen is made up of an overall assessment of experiences the singular individual, or several, has had in a number of circumstances that have to do with the event. These experiences can be marked on a continuum scale to illustrate or make concrete how unexpected the event was. The marking can be done with a cross, or perhaps preferably, by way of oval circles as Figure 5.1 illustrates.

All these factors will have a different degree of the unforeseen. Thus, they are key factors as bases for the planning of learning and training for the unforeseen, and can be injected as a part of the script and varied in and during the training and learning process. In this regard, the didactic Bow-tie model (Figure 1.1) can be of help in expressing the learning plan. TU-oriented training has three didactic approaches: (1) *Intended* (known to the directing staff or teachers – unknown to the participants or students), (2) *Spontaneous* (unknown to all, e.g. in a learning or training situation to be productive moments) and (3) *Hybrid* (planning for possible spontaneous and unannounced situations that are explored in other intended scripts).

Degree of the Unforeseen
Continuum field

	An event			
Extreme point	Overall – High Degree of Unforeseen	Overall – Medium Degree of Unforeseen	Overall – Low Degree of Unforeseen	*Extreme point*
Total unlikely	←		→	Total likely
Total unknown	←		→	Total known
0 warning time	←		→	Max warning time
0 Sign	←		→	Max number of signs

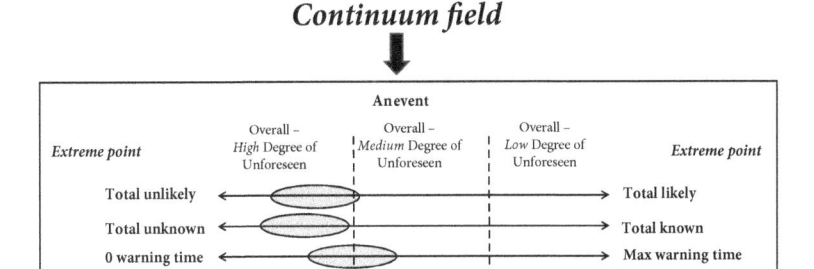

Figure 5.1 Degree of the unforeseen, expressed by an overall assessment of experiences for four TU-factors on a continuum scale, which is divided into three main degrees: high, medium and low (these can also be divided into several units). In the example, the overall perceived degree of the unforeseen, that is, the sum of all factors, would be high, meaning a high degree of the unforeseen (modified after Saeverot & Torgersen, 2024).

Strategic didatic TU model

Based on our findings in the TU research, we have developed such a new planning model for learning and training skills to develop better preparedness for unforeseen events. It is called the 'Strategic Didactic TU model' (SD-TU model) (Torgersen & Saeverot, 2015).

The didactic planning model for TU-learning (Figure 5.2) complements learning goals with generic competence areas, like self-efficacy, social support, improvisation and interaction. New studies (Torgersen, 2018) implicate that interaction is one of the most distinct predictors for handling unforeseen events. However, the concept of interaction is here based on a high relationally level of ambitions, different from traditionally 'cooperation', and consists of something more than, for example, communication and coordination. Interaction under risk and unpredictable conditions presupposes emphasizing on other factors than what is the case for interaction when conducted under predictable conditions. For example, one should emphasize on educational structures (e.g. extract knowledge out from disorder in information and surroundings), organizational structures (e.g. shared leadership, the avoidance of organizational narcissism) and operational structures (e.g. collective acceptance for immediate trust and loss of control). The pedagogical approach should be indirect (Saeverot, 2013; 2022b), and use of 'invisible methods', which implies minimum use of defined blueprint solutions, and a conscious use of unclear learning content.

The core of the Strategic Didactic TU model is that all didactic choices that occur during a planning process for the design of training plans and training schemes require that assessments are related to competence structures that are assumed to be relevant in the event of unforeseen events. These competence structures replace the specific learning objectives, which are not known in the event of unforeseen events.

The competence structures are outlined at the bottom of Figure 5.2, in line with the Danish innovation educator, Lotte Darsø's (2012) terminology 'knowledge' and 'non-knowledge' in her 'innovation diamond'. In addition, preparedness has specific frameworks and goals, which must be taken into account in the didactic reflections. This is in addition to ordinary framework factors, such as available time for the training, teaching rooms, equipment and other general resources needed to carry out training and exercises (Torgersen, 2015).

Such a way of planning competence development to meet unforeseen events will affect the way preparedness exercises and other learning programs are carried out, both at the planning stage and in practice, and not least in connection with quality assessments and improvement processes. The interaction factor is crucial in all TU training.

The model (Figure 5.2) corrects the potential weaknesses of the traditional didactic relation model (Saeverot & Torgersen, 2022) and also the 'didactic relation model for adult education' (Loeng et al., 2001), when using them as didactic planning tools for learning how to handle unforeseen events. Among others, learning objectives, which will be unknown or extremely ambiguous, are replaced in competency training for unforeseen events. Consequently, the traditional didactic

Didactic Models for the Unforeseen 77

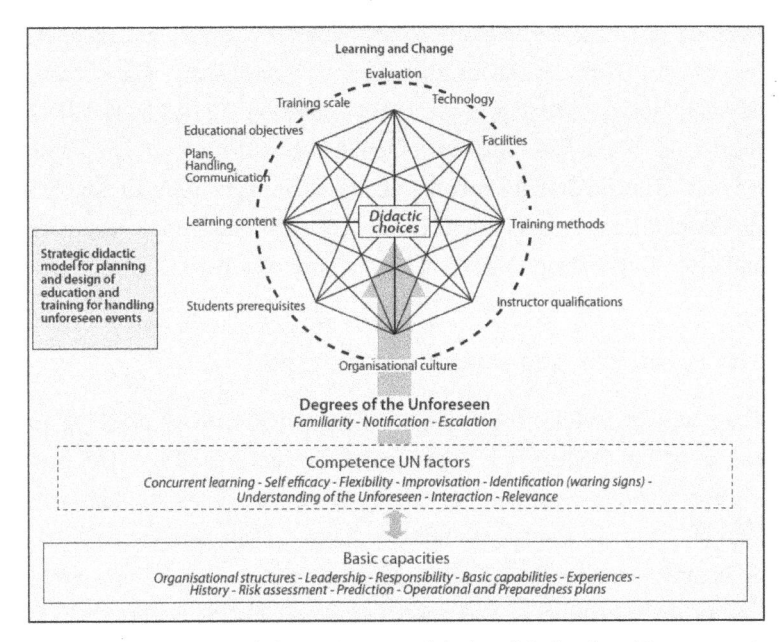

Figure 5.2 Strategic didactic TU model (modified after Torgersen & Saeverot, 2015, p. 330). It is a relational model, where traditional detailed learning goals, which are not comprehensively known during training for TU, are replaced with identified overall knowledge structures, given by TU relations and basic relations.

relation model is under pressure when subjected to such prerequisites. In all likelihood, particularly due to the basic causal structure of the model between the factors, it may not be possible to use this 'relational' thinking at all. Despite this, we do not currently have grounds to fully reject the relational principles except for proposing some adjustments in the factor content and their meaning. The relational principle also remains extremely current in crisis management literature.

A relational approach is therefore the main principle in the SD-TU model, whereby the 'diamond structure' of the model corresponds to the interactive structure of the 'Diamond Model of Crisis Management: Interactive Systems Thinking' (Mitroff et al., 2004, p. 177). In Scandinavian pedagogy, such a 'diamond' structure is also often used to express the connection between overall factors which are important for planning teaching in school and education, and how these factors are mutually dependent. In particular, factors such as learning goals, learning conditions, learning processes, setting, content and evaluation are highlighted. This means that all the factors have a mutually interacting impact, and if one factor is changed, it will affect the others accordingly. Such an adjusted model may be an alternative until research can justify and document other and better ways of planning and designing such education.

Main principles and concepts of the model

The result of a didactic process, that is, activities from planning to execution and evaluation, is 'learning and changes' (Table 5.1). This goal involves learning in connection with the education process, in addition to learning that may generate the need for strategic change, changed actions or organization. Deficiencies and weaknesses can often be uncovered during the execution of education processes. It is then important to take these seriously and use them as a basis for assessments, potential adjustments and changes. Another important element is that the learning culture is not characterized by a 'scapegoat culture'. The organization

Table 5.1 Overview of the content and meaning of the various didactic categories in an expanded didactic relation model for education, as a basis for didactic decisions related to the unforeseen (the outer circle in Figure 5.2) (modified after Torgersen & Saeverot, 2015, pp. 331–6)

Category	Short description of the categories/didactic factors
Didactic decision	All necessary assessments are carried out in connection with planning, executing and evaluating education. When making such decisions, all relevant conditions are compared to each other, and the consequences and alternatives are assessed to determine the best outcome with the highest possible pedagogical quality for the students.
Learning and changes	The purpose of the education is learning in connection with the education process, in addition to learning which may generate the need for changes to the education on the whole, or strategies and actions of the organization.

Category	Short description of the categories/didactic factors
Evaluation	Evaluation after completion of the education or training process or along the way (process evaluation). Development and use of relevant methods to test competencies or ways to construct examinations/tests in view of unforeseen events.
Technology	Specific technological and digital aids in connection with the education and training, for example, specific ICT and software, simulators, communication equipment; transport, medical, weaponry or robot technology included in the education.
Framework factors	Time, premises, field, materials, access to personnel and other resources that are needed for or contribute to influencing the design and execution of the education.
Working methods	Teaching and supervision methods, ways to organize the teaching/lessons/education. All approaches should be considered, however, emphasis should be placed on indirect methods that do not require ritual acts and solutions, but bring forth improvisation, self-insight, collaboration and creative processes, to utilize the productive moments in the teaching.
Ability of instructors	Professional and pedagogical competence of the instructor/plan developer and others connected to the education. Perhaps these should be educated first? Good knowledge of the concept TU, its nature and content.
Culture	The workplace or school culture among the teachers, instructors, participants, aspects of a professional culture, for example, safety culture, knowledge of the network structure of the organization, attitude towards education, etc. This factor also strongly impacts the development of an education design for the unforeseen; however, an understanding of one's own organization will also be necessary, which in this context is virtually a separate learning objective. For example, an understanding of the principle of adapted education for all children and pupils in kindergarten and school will be important for school leaders, teachers (and also parents and the pupils) attached to this.
Ability of participants	Previous knowledge, experience, the knowledge and motivation of the participants/pupils (target group), knowledge of the relevant pedagogical working methods that will be used in the education (should training for this also be given first?).

(*Continued*)

Category	Short description of the categories/didactic factors
Content	Professional content, themes, progression, sequencing of themes (how much at a time) and what the participators will encounter in the learning situation. The content is also closely related to the selected tiers of the unforeseen. Whenever new content appears suddenly and unexpectedly, a systematic sequencing or progression will be possible. This must be accepted by teachers and school leaders.
Planning, management, communication (types of emergency preparedness in school and education)	Main tool for the education in relation to the function of emergency preparedness in educational institutions: *Planning*: that is, the quality of emergency preparedness plans and development, and degree of inclusion in ordinary curricula. *Management*: involves the development of competency for mastering unforeseen events during the process as it is happening, including the identification of escalation, management as it unfolds and the normalization phases afterwards. *Communication*: in connection with both the first two types, that is, operational crisis communication and management of the media and society in connection with crises, so-called strategic and tactical crisis communication.
Goals	Various types of competency goals (learning objectives or competence goals) related to the education, goal level (main/sub-goal) and the type of competency they should describe (e.g. main goal, sub-goal, cognitive goal, affective/attitude goal, psychomotor/skills goal, social/relational goal). In the SD-TU model, this type of 'goal' is largely unknown or ambiguous. This factor is therefore replaced or supplemented by a combination of more aggregated competencies related to 'Basic Relations', 'TU Knowledge' and organizational circumstances such as 'scales'. However, any known goals (experiences) should also be assessed.
Scales (desktop, function, full scale)	The scope of the education and how much the education should resemble reality: (1) Desktop (computer/paper-based training), (2) function-oriented (competency aimed at specific work tasks/work processes or functions or parts thereof) and (3) full scale (whole schools and cooperative networks are practised).

should instead emphasize learning from one's mistakes. We have placed this main objective at the top of the model.

Traditional 'part' and 'TU-oriented learning habits'

At the core of the SD-TU model is that all didactic decisions that are made in a design planning process for training curricula and training programmes assume that assessments are related to the competency structures considered relevant to the unforeseen event. The competency structures replace the concrete learning objectives (goals) which, in terms of unforeseen events, are not known. In this context, it is important that the school's leaders, teachers, parents and not least the students themselves understand and accept that 'good' and learning-rich teaching can also take place without clear learning objectives, precisely in order to make use of spontaneous situations and events. In order to achieve this, spontaneous learning without predetermined objectives should be included in the school's national and local curricula, and also in the teacher training courses. In addition, such type of education should be used over time. Not everyone has belief in such unorthodox types of education right away. We call this 'TU-oriented learning habits' about the learning process and the lack of clear learning objectives under unforeseen conditions.

The competency structures are outlined at the bottom of Figure 5.2 under competency categories 'Basic Relations' (knowledge) and 'TU Relations' (no knowledge). Additionally, emergency preparedness has distinctive frameworks and goals which must also be incorporated into didactic reflection. These are in addition to the ordinary 'framework factors' (in the model, Figure 5.2), such as available time for the education, classroom, equipment and other general resources that are necessary for executing the education, supervision and exercises.

Known competencies

When planning education to build competency for unforeseen events, it is necessary to develop and secure basic competency to handle familiar and unforeseen events. This competency category is referred to as 'Knowledge Competency' in line with Lotte Darsøs terminology (2012) in her 'Diamond of Innovation'. This category is outlined at the bottom of the above model (Figure 5.2) with nine competency structures (Table 5.2).

Table 5.2 Competency structures in the category 'Knowledge Competency' (modified after Torgersen & Saeverot, 2015, pp. 334–5)

Concept	Competency structure
Organizational structure	How the institution (e.g. the educational institution) is organized (design) and adapted to the tasks, and potential relationships between other cooperative institutions, including emergency preparedness organizations.
Leadership	How the educational institutions' management is executed, command and communication lines, delegation and how these relate to the external institutions, including emergency preparedness organization.
Responsibility	The relationship between responsibility and authority, and how this relates to the external institutions, including emergency preparedness organization.
Basic capabilities	Access to learning material resources, supplies, logistics and the competency to act and manage them accordingly, and to, inter alia, use tools and procedures, as well as mental preparedness, for example, self-insight and a sense of mastery, during familiar events.
Experiences	The experience base of the organization, storage system and exploitation of earlier experiences from events involving the organization for learning purposes (direct experiential learning).
History	The storage system of the organization for events in which the organization was not necessarily directly involved, and exploitation of this for learning purposes (indirect experiential learning).
Risk assessment	The competency of the organization to assess risk both before and during events.

Concept	Competency structure
Prediction	The competency of the organization to assess the probability of future events and its perception of the reliability of prediction as a tool.
Plans	The strategic education plan and curricula and the extent to which these are adapted and including operational and emergency preparedness plans of the organization and correlation between them, the degree to which the various plans contain descriptions of relevant circumstances related to unforeseen events, and whether the various plans have the same aims. Are these plans well known in the organization, updated and, not least, have various types of exercises been carried out in accordance with the plans – and unforeseen events (the plans should include a section for 'What is unknown').

The expression 'Basic Capabilities' innately gives access to learning materials, resources, supplies, logistics and the competency to act and manage them accordingly, and to, inter alia, use tools, procedures and mental preparedness, for example, self-insight and a sense of mastery, during familiar events. In other words, this is a form of basic competency and general material resources that should be fundamental in all types of events, both in schools, other workplaces and in the society.

What is unknown

It is essential to relate didactic reflection to competency areas that are considered crucial for the management of unforeseen events. In the model, this competency category is referred to as 'No Knowledge' and 'TU Relations', and it contains eight competency structures (Table 5.3). These competency structures are based on the main characteristics of other competency areas mentioned in this book and experiences from serious events.

However, those who will be handling the situation will always attach a different tier of unforeseeability to the event. As we have seen earlier, the tier of expected unforeseeability for the participators is acted out as part of a lesson plan in scenarios, simulations and exercises. Additionally, the alert level for both a complete exercise and individual parts along the way could be controlled in connection with didactic planning. This is frequently referred to as alerted and unalerted exercises. The same applies to the level of information and signs given in connection with escalation of events during an exercise (warning signs). These are unique didactic factors in education design for managing unforeseen events.

The tiers of unforeseeability (Table 5.4) for 'familiarity', 'alerting' and 'warning signs' should therefore be assessed in combination with the

Table 5.3 Competency structures in the category 'No Knowledge' (modified after Torgersen & Saeverot, 2015, pp. 335–6)

Concept	Competency structure
Concurrent learning/Learning along the way	The competency of the actors (school leaders, teachers, pupils and students) to observe, register, communicate and exploit relevant details during events. The ability or capacity to memorize the present.
Self-efficacy	The competency of the actors to assess their own capacity to cope and sense of mastery.
Flexibility	The capability of the actors and organization to change procedures and ways of acting along the way in situations.
Improvisation	The competency of the actors to find new and unfamiliar solutions along the way in an ambiguous and complex situation.
Identification (signs)	The competency of the actors and organization to retrieve, register and communicate warning (or positive) signs of potential future events (foresight).

Concept	Competency structure
Understanding TU	The awareness and understanding of the organization with regard to what the unforeseen means to the organization or a written down definition or explanation in plans made known to all people in the organization, collaborating organizations and networks (e.g. in connection with outsourced enterprises).
Interaction	The competency of the actors to exchange and complement each other's competencies during education and events.
Relevance	Emphasis on unforeseen relevance. Assessment of what might be relevant content and methods for education and training on how to master unforeseen events. Assessing relevance is in itself an important competency, for example, the degree to which experiential learning, improvisation and the principle of 'train as you fight' (emergency) is the best method in relation to building competency to master unforeseen events.

Table 5.4 Competency structures in the category 'Tiers of Unforeseeability' (modified after Torgersen & Saeverot, 2015, pp. 336)

Concept	Competency structure
Familiarity	The extent to which an event is expected to be familiar to participants in a learning sequence.
Notification	The degree to which and in what way information is given about an event incorporated into an education programme or exercise before the event occurs in a pedagogical sequence.
Escalation	The degree to which information is given to signal escalation of an event in a learning sequence, which may train participators to identify the (warning) signs and choose potential measures.

principles for 'Knowledge' and 'No Knowledge', and as relational factors of the didactic decisions and factors included therein. In the SD-TU model (Figure 5.2), these variables are specified between the relational factors for didactic decisions and the competency databases below.

Critical use of the SD-TU model and reverse didactic degree

The SD-TU model may constitute a holistic didactic model for strategic planning of education intended to develop relevant competencies for managing unforeseen events when the learning objective is unknown. As such, it can be used when developing both strategic education and training curricula, and more concrete teaching and training programmes. Training and practice are needed in order to make use of this model in practice. That will be a task for both the teacher training programs and the authorities.

Nonetheless, one should be aware of the weaknesses of such a model in view of the nature of TU. Even though a lot of resources are allocated to education and training it will never be fully possible to cover the competency that is actually required when an event occurs. Despite this, we still believe that such a model (developed on the basis of the nature of the TU concept) can be a better alternative than models that require linearity and learning objectives with familiar and unambiguous content.

Key to the model is an evaluation of the varying degrees of un-expectedness of phenomena that should be learnt in light of risks and potential threats, while traditionally defined learning objectives are replaced by more generic knowledge such as interaction, improvisation, confidence in own abilities and self-insight. Yet even this model requires a relationship between the planning factors. For that reason this model, too, has some weaknesses when unforeseen events are factored in. One of the main reasons for the model's shortcomings is that the risk aspect and potential threats are clearly incorporated into the model as a prerequisite.

In addition, it will be important that teachers and education authorities are aware of the effect of what we term 'the reverse didactic degree'. This term means as follows: the more unforeseen and spontaneous events that are utilized and drawn into the teaching, the less control the teacher will have over the learning outcome of the teaching. Biesta's (2015) concept of the risk of education can be of relevance here. Furthermore, in connection with exercises, perhaps related to preparedness, input of unforeseen events in the exercises themselves, may increase the risk that dangerous situations for both people and equipment involved could in fact occur, precisely because the didactic control decreases. In other words, the reverse didactic degree means thus: higher degree of unpredictability in the teaching plan or the exercises will lower the didactic control over the situation during the course and the learning outcome.

Didactic Balance Model

In Saeverot and Torgersen (2022), we therefore developed a didactic model for how we, to the extent possible, could remove the assumptions and also avoid establishing traditional relationships between certain factors. This would require a new and innovative didactic perspective. Instead of focusing on typical didactic categories such as relationships, goals or content, we shifted our attention to balance, with two possible end points in a continuum (see Figure 5.3).

This model has a 'balance point', a sort of 'golden middle ground' rather than facilitating a bias towards either value perspective. Reflexive judgment is key to this model, where we are made aware of potential forces towards certain perspectives as part of the reflection, and as a basis for further learning and development. The purpose is to develop reflexive judgement, which in turn would contribute to development

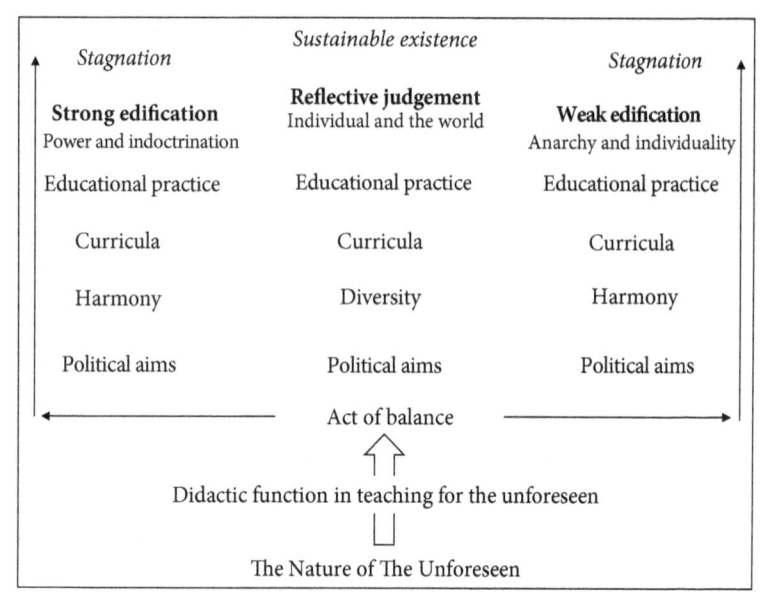

Stagnation	Sustainable existence	Stagnation
Strong edification Power and indoctrination	**Reflective judgement** Individual and the world	**Weak edification** Anarchy and individuality
Educational practice	Educational practice	Educational practice
Curricula	Curricula	Curricula
Harmony	Diversity	Harmony
Political aims	Political aims	Political aims

← Act of balance →

Didactic function in teaching for the unforeseen

The Nature of The Unforeseen

Figure 5.3 Didactic Balance Model (DBM-model). Modified after Saeverot & Torgersen, 2022; 2024.

and sustainability rather than threats. However, if pedagogical practice is solely aimed at one of the end points, this would also limit the learning to a specific direction or ideology.

When viewed in relation to the development of reflexive judgement, this would involve a stagnation of the learning development. This occurs because the underlying learning process has been bound within a framework and would therefore be based on fear and power.

Both fear and power can occur at the two end points, with a balanced centre point. At the one end point (to the left of the model), there could be a strong formative education, which could also be called indoctrination, meaning bound by power.

At the other end point (to the right of the model), the underlying learning processes would be absolutely free, without any form of facilitation or organized content. In this way, the education would be similarly bound by freedom, where whatever is based on fear and power consists of a fear of losing this absolute freedom. Here, there is a weak education process, even if it is strongly individual-oriented. Thus, we would have a form of liberation under power, where power is based on maintaining absolute freedom.

Both outcomes would result in the stagnation of learning development. Under such conditions and standardizations, perspectives and ideologies would develop that could threaten the quality of existence.

Between these two end points, at the balance point, we would find a sustainable development of life and existence for both the individual and the world. Here, the model opens for an existence that respects life, which occurs via reflexive judgement. This existence may arise because the education involves liberation without power. We must emphasize that the specific balance point would in practice depend on local conditions, and therefore, we must identify these balance points, assess them and give them content in every education and school.

In light of the pedagogy for the unforeseen, there may be several potential balance points that could lead to reflexive judgement, learning and development. We will look at four examples of such balance points, which again appear as examples of didactic planning factors for judgment and knowledge development (Saeverot & Torgersen, 2024).

Balance point 1: Political goals

The education system is largely built on political ideas (balance point 1), which in turn are embodied in curricula and teacher education programmes, and which also govern a teacher's pedagogical practices.

One solution to this may be to make students, school leaders, politicians and others aware of the possible political and ideological guidelines that form the foundation for the education and discuss the consequences of these, without giving primacy to specific guidelines, if possible.

Balance point 2: Harmony and diversity

Standardizations, with a focus on certain guiding ideologies, would provide a sense of harmony, but at the same time this harmony presupposes the exclusion of other approaches. The alternative is a focus on diversity and the awareness of different ideologies and perspectives, which may also involve a sense of freedom and harmony but without excluding other ideologies.

Balance point 3: Curricula

The hierarchical plan for educational activities would be important for the selection of content, and for how to facilitate and evaluate these pedagogically. Local curricula built on central curricula from governing authorities (cf. balance point 1). For individual schools and teachers, local curricula would be local governing documents, which would therefore also have a concrete impact on pedagogical practices.

Here, individual schools and teachers may often have the opportunity to influence the content to a certain extent. This may lead to individual solutions, which in turn could contribute to an emphasis on certain perspectives of importance for the balance point.

Balance point 4: Pedagogical practice

This model allows teachers to consistently balance their instruction based on a balance point and end points, to ensure that they are aware that their chosen form of teaching allows for a sustainable pedagogy. This implies a pedagogical practice where students can be independent and free.

Without the awareness permitted by this model, teachers risk nearing one of the end points. This may result in a pedagogical practice where teachers steer students in certain directions, both in terms of knowledge acquisition and practicing skills.

6

The Unforeseen and New Forms of Terrorism

Introduction

Digital media is and will probably be used even more in the future to spread extreme ideological messages, and as an instrument in relation to terror attacks and other violent and unforeseen acts. This especially applies to so-called solo actor terrorists or 'lone wolf terrorists', who carry out brutal acts by simple means with somewhat little planning and few people. The following is an example: In contrast to the Oklahoma City bomber (19 April 1995), social media was used as a tool to spread extreme ideological messages in connection with the attacks on Norwegian territory on 22 July 2011. We have also seen that freedom of speech may be under threat due to multiple recent terrorist acts, and the threat picture is continually changing in its form and character, which also includes digital and visual media. Society faces hybrid threats (HT), which by their nature are composite and unpredictable. The attackers will exploit vulnerabilities and challenges, both in children, in schools and in society as a whole. Digital attacks are examples. It creates new didactic challenges for teachers and school authorities.

Sensible vigilance and digital awakening

We therefore ask how a modern democratic society can build up competencies and mental preparedness that can both prevent the development of extreme acts and at the same time help to uncover the escalation of such acts. In his New Year speech (1 January 2012), the prime minister at that time, Jens Stoltenberg, used the expression 'digital nosy neighbours' to portray that everyone must pay close attention to potential threats via the internet and otherwise in society. In other words, it is important to develop what we describe as *sensible vigilance*. By this, we mean that each person should be vigilant towards potential threats in a way that does not limit our freedom to act, or attention to daily chores and the use of technology, or prevent us from living in accordance with the democratic values and principles we appreciate. In order to develop such competencies, a new form of pedagogy should also be developed for use in schools and other training and education institutions to approach what we have described earlier as 'digital awakening' (Torgersen & Saeverot, 2011; 2012). Digital awakening must not, however, be understood as a concrete pedagogical method with definitive answers for learning or education. On the contrary, the term must be understood as a contribution to more democratic awareness, and fundamental thinking on which practical pedagogy can be built to precisely realize this. To expand on this further, two key conditions related to terrorism in modern times are used as a point of departure: (1) terrorism's rate of change and (2) virtual terrorism.

Terrorism's rate of change

The terrorist acts against the World Trade Center in New York on 11 September 2001 changed the worldview, especially in relation to security behaviour and social infrastructure worldwide, but also in relation to language, rhetoric, intelligence and the individual's alertness to extreme ideological groups (Mueller, 2012). These events were incorporated as themes at all levels in the education systems and became the object of research in various disciplines and approaches. Despite this, the terrorist acts on 22 July 2011 came like a bolt out of the blue for the Norwegian society and the world at large. There was no continuity between the acts, that is, systematic and continuous escalation, which could directly predict the attacks. Such unforeseen and surprising incidents are therefore discontinuous in nature. In turn, this will create fear. We end up with a so-called Risk Society (Beck, 1992), which challenges the democratic worldview.

For this reason, there is a need to develop and raise awareness of the individual's power of judgement and ability to identify with societal development trends and potential risk of ideological-based acts of violence. In connection with this, we underline the need for proactive and education-oriented 'measures', which in practice may correspond to the metaphor 'digital nosy neighbours' – expressed by Prime Minister Jens Stoltenberg in his New Year speech on 1 January 2012. Schools and the education system must address this with adequate pedagogical approaches and thematic choices that can give pupils and students not only fact-based knowledge about the events but also sufficient critical skills that will enable them to detect extreme ideological messages and threats, which are constantly changing in their communication form, action pattern and character. Michael A. Peters clarifies this:

> Terrorism, whether domestic or international – and increasingly in a borderless world the line is harder to draw – tends to be neither left or right but rather ethnic and separatist. Postmodern terrorism seemingly has no limits, no inside or outside: it is transnational, truly global, highly mobile, and cellular. It makes use of new global technologies in communication and information-exchange: cells are 'intelligent networks' able to conduct surveillance, decode and hack into official systems and databases. (…) Postmodern terrorism is also telegenic: it is aware that wars and terrorism must use the media in all its forms to shape the subjectivities of the viewing public.
>
> (Peters, 2008)

No specific and consistent social or psychological development characteristics, so-called 'routes' towards active terrorism, have been identified either (Taylor & Horgan, 2012). On the contrary, it concerns individual and special life routes where the individual or groups change over time in the direction of planning and carrying out acts of terrorism (Taylor & Horgan, 2012) That is to say, there are no defined common characteristics between background and acts of terrorism, which makes it impossible to predict the tendency of violent terrorism based on specific social or psychological development trends. A fixed and absolute answer for what terrorism is, who represents a threat, and how it can be detected, may therefore be contrary to the objective. Instead, a form of pedagogy is needed that will allow each individual's engagement, reflection and judgement, and insight into the fundamental principles of democracy.

Virtual terrorism

Terrorism expert and former Deputy Assistant Secretary of State Steve R. Pieczenik, who had special responsibility for terrorism issues under five American presidents, believes that the person charged for the attacks in Norway on 22 July 2011 differs from earlier terrorists by his extensive use of twenty-first-century instruments. Pieczenik therefore claims that these acts should be looked at in view of twenty-first-century technology, particularly Facebook, Twitter and other social communication media (EFG-BN, 2011). He describes the phenomenon as virtual terrorism. This means that the various internet-based mediatization channels are used to express extreme ideological ideas and manifestos. An important factor is that these media can use all representational forms: audio, images, videos, text and interactivity, both separately and in combination. This makes the media inclusive and activating. At the same time, the imagery and combination of the representational forms encourage both sharp concretization and clarification of the message in a direct manner, and a multitude of possibilities for tactical use of visual and verbal metaphors and analogies to indirectly sneak in a message. Concurrently, the media are tactically used by competent ideological groups as an instrument in their political, religious and ideological marketing and indoctrination.

Additionally, these forms of media are mainly used and developed by the internet generation (iGen): children, adolescents and young adults. The iGen has grown up with these media, which have been a key factor in their formation. This means that extreme attitudes and ideological messages mediatized via these channels may over time be perceived as ordinary, thus rendering the message and its consequences harmless – even if the main message encourages violence and terrorism. Thus, the message does not necessarily create fear, rejection or aggregation of critical attitudes towards the content among the recipients. Such generalization involves a form of thematic or substantive habit with the most extreme consequence potentially leading to indifference and a form of passive acceptance.

This can also be compared to psychological adaptation processes in relation to how cinematic effects have developed over time from, for example, classical black-and-white science-fiction films from the 1950s, or colour reproduction of that time, to today's high-tech films with associated compositions and effects. The youth of today are unlikely to be captivated by the classics in the same way as earlier generations, and these films have now been downgraded in terms of age limits. Such adaptation is incorporated into the formation process and becomes a key component in the formation of attitudes and ideological development. Traditional thinking around the role of schools in developing the digital literacy of pupils must therefore be reassessed and given a new pedagogical platform and direction for something concrete and action oriented. At the same time, the learning processes must be indirect and less based on frameworks and answer sheets.

The military has a long tradition of using audio and pictorial media as pedagogical tools in education and training (Torgersen, 2008). This is done to grasp reality and to transmit this as a point of departure for education and training. This falls under the pedagogical principle of the military to 'train as you fight'. Nonetheless, it is equally important to train for unforeseen events and situations where no correct answers or procedures have been given in advance. In this respect, the use of images and videos also has important pedagogical functions. Additionally, images may contribute to a common language across borders. This is important for collaboration and the education of multinational groups, both civilian and military. All-encompassing and critical-oriented education is also necessary in the civilian education system. This assumes that the teachers have pedagogical insight into this. In our view, we shall argue that the didactic consequences of education are a key factor.

Problem

Based on this, 'someone' must contribute to competent digital awakening, that is, raise awareness of these processes to build up critical skills that can aggregate and uncover messages conveyed through social media. Schools will play an important role in this in the future. The question is whether such digital awakening can be achieved through traditional media education and methods for text and image analyses. At the same time, it is necessary that educational leaders and practising teachers contribute to a competent understanding of democracy and world citizenship. We therefore ask the following question: How can this form of pedagogy be firmly rooted and implemented in practice?

To approach the above main question, we are using the following question as a basis: Is the pedagogical awakening or the education process continuous or discontinuous? The discussion from this part may provide necessary conceptual clarification and theoretical foundation to suggest how the practical implementation of education may take place: How can education contribute to digital awakening in practice?

Continuous and discontinuous awakening

Awakening from digital slumber

In his collection of essays, *Existenzphilosophie und Pädagogik. Versuch über unstetige Formen der Erziehung* (1959/77), Otto Friedrich Bollnow differentiates between several stages or levels of analogous states from which a (pedagogical) awakening can spring. Here he points to the notion of 'slumber', which is a mental state between sleep and wakefulness. This state can also be characterized by indifference to the environment or a state of non-involvement or reflection on the message one is facing. We believe that this type of 'digital slumber' is a state that may over time occur when the iGen encounter extreme messages via social media. Digital awakening therefore involves a conscious awakening from digital slumber to uncover and raise awareness of the content of messages after which personal reflection and vigilance leading to digital wakefulness may begin. Such personal reflection will involve a justified stance on the content, rejection and distancing or approval, at the same time as mental alertness is established with regard to hidden extreme messages and acts. In our democratic society, rooted in a philosophy on world citizenship (which harkens back to Immanuel Kant's cosmopolitan ideal), our concern is that digital awakening will contribute to the rejection of extreme ideologies that use violence and terrorism as instruments even though it may, to some degree, involve a normative approach towards the awakening process.

Nonetheless, is the process from digital slumber via the awakening phase up to digital wakefulness a continuous or discontinuous process? Bollnow argues that an educational awakening, almost on par with a religious revival, is a discontinuous process (Bollnow, 1959/1977). This is because in relation to time, a mental awakening is an abrupt process where one suddenly understands, becomes aware of or uncovers a factual situation. In this respect, the awakening occurs from a state where the individual was previously inactive, uninvolved or not engaged – or had no knowledge thereof. According to Bollnow's approach, a classical educational awakening does not imply renewal of an earlier conscious state, but a new state completely separated from the former. As such, the awakened state is not only new but also ends when a potential new awakening occurs. This kind of awakening is therefore discontinuous.

Digital awakening, the development of insight and problem of continuity

Digital awakening, however, is both a continuous and discontinuous process. It is continuous because digital slumber, in contrast to general educational slumber, as Bollnow (1959/1977) described this state, is based on well-established practices and knowledge, and understanding of both technology and messages as forms. As previously mentioned, this means that the iGen is familiar with the social media; they master the technical features and use them in their daily communication with others. At the same time, it is likely that they know about terrorism, the use of violence as a method, and that the internet is used to spread extreme ideological messages. At least, this applies to slightly older children and adolescents, who are or have been pupils in organized school systems familiar to us in the Western world. There are probably few schools that have not had this as a theme in various subjects and projects. However, this daily use and teaching may contribute to making this a common theme in line with other subjects and topics, and on par with other socialization factors that young people are very familiar with. Digital awakening therefore relates to the ongoing story along with the user or pupil where adaptation and mastery of the technology as a communication form is incorporated and used as a foundation (digital literacy). This is a continuous process.

A digital awakening will therefore occur continuously over time, and inevitably with other educational approaches compared to traditional subjects and topics. Concurrently, the raising of awareness or 'awakening' of events and experiences conveyed via different media also has a discontinuous nature. This happens when the raising of awareness is transformed into insight, which includes independent valuation and taking a stance on the message, and the visual and verbal instruments that are used. The transition from digital slumber and habit-oriented perception of mediatized messages to the transformed state of awareness involves an abrupt mental transition where the new state is qualitatively different from the previous one. Such a discontinuous process can only occur as a consequence of self-reflection with or without 'external' initiators. An external initiator could be educational programmes in schools, but also sudden events in society. Let us first look into the latter based on Bollnow's (1959/1977) five main characteristics or prerequisites for 'awakening'.

- The person to be awakened must have the potential for the awakening he/she is about to have.
- The process can only be induced by external initiators.
- The process involves a certain degree of violence where one is pulled out of a state of stagnation, and the awakening is therefore always a painful experience.
- Outside influences lead to a crisis-like process associated with a radical change from a state of inauthenticity to a state of authenticity.
- A period of wakefulness and growth (after awakening).

In our view, the attacks in Norway on 22 July 2011 are an example of 'external' events corresponding to Bollnow's prerequisites for awakening. Rhetorical analysis also demonstrates that the political environments and the Norwegian population at large changed the way they talked and had an inclination to immediately use ritual actions. For example, the use of language both privately and publicly took on the tone of more absolute democratic statements. Words such as 'charity', 'care' and 'tolerance' were frequently used by the media and politicians. At the same time, grief and a sense of community were expressed through basic rituals such as laying down flowers. Thus, attention to extreme statements and messages mediatized via social media was completely different than earlier. The content of the message received a new and concrete meaning. A discontinuous awakening and insight into the content of this type of message had occurred. How can such awakening be put into pedagogical practice?

How can education contribute to awakening in practice?

As previously mentioned, we do not believe that digital awakening can be achieved through traditional media education and exegetic methods for text and image analyses. But why not?

Digital awakening through exegetic approaches?

The pedagogical challenge is to get pupils to want to take the leap from a state of slumber to awareness independently. In our view, traditional cooperative learning, media education and exegetic methods are little equipped to achieve this. The reason being that the primary purpose of these methods is to find a specific message. The reference frame for the content of the message is provided by the methods, for example, semiotic picture analysis or discourse analysis. When looking at this in the context of schools, the teacher will be the reference frame, that is, a frame that is not only limited by the teacher's competency but also the solutions that are delimited by correct answers – directly through specific proposed solutions from the teacher or from others the teacher applauds. This gives an authoritative stamp to follow, which the pupils can measure their performance and solutions up against. With this type of reference point during development, the pupils will remain in an existential state of slumber even if they have solved the tasks correctly using the correct methods. Consequently, they will not achieve new insight, which is a prerequisite for digital awakening. Digital awakening does not occur as a consequence of actions as per predetermined procedures, but by following an approach the individual has discovered themselves. Cooperative learning is not a satisfactory method in this context either, as it concerns development of solutions in fellowship. Each pupil has to put their trust in others, which prevents awakening from the state of slumber.

However, knowledge and skills developed through traditional learning processes and working methods may be one of several solutions to the awakening process. Therefore, we also point out the role of schools in this context. Nonetheless, teaching should first and foremost facilitate the attainment of insight through an indirect form of pedagogy (Saeverot, 2022b) where pupils find solutions that they perceive as their own, and which can form the basis for an individual awakening process.

Digital awakening through indirect pedagogy

In other words, pupils can be awakened through a pedagogical approach, but the approach cannot be carried out in a direct way; it must be done indirectly. Bollnow seems to support this by referring to Eduard Spranger: With regard to the concept of awakening, Spranger states that it is not 'about a pedagogical technique that can calculate its effects' (Bollnow, 1959/1977, p. 85). The pedagogical standpoint of Spranger implies that the teacher cannot resort to giving a direct message, which leads to a specific type of awakening. The teacher must therefore communicate in an indirect way, that is, a communication form that does not steer pupils in an unambiguous direction but touches their state of slumber in such a way that he or she begins to reflect and thereafter achieves new awareness.

In the extension of indirect pedagogy, we believe that the use of images and pictorial media may contribute to a pedagogical awakening process in light of digital awakening. In terms of emotions and situations, images have a unique activating quality. We do not think, however, that the use of classical image and text analysis methods is the only route to take. Free associations related to what images and text mean to the individual should also be facilitated. This can also be done in connection with discussions around 'hate speech' (Nielsen, 2014), for example, on social media. However, as soon as 'formal' frameworks for interpreting images and text are introduced, the discovery and educational effects are reduced. The use of images and text as a door opener directly into the individual's experiences, understanding and insight may be one step in the right direction and a 'method' for initiating (refer to external initiators) both continuous and discontinuous awakening processes of uncovering, taking a stance and insight. That is to say, a digital awakening of extreme ideological messages mediatized through 'familiar' social media.

Schools of the future

Proposed fixed solutions and determination of the nature of terrorism may in our argument be contrary to the objective. The pupils become locked within their mental insight and will be unable to follow the constantly changing and unforeseen faces of terrorism. Nonetheless, an indirect form of pedagogy may touch the pupils, enabling them to be guided out of a half-awaken state of slumber to reflect and further awaken to awareness and insight. This form of pedagogy is not unequivocally continuous nor is it unequivocally discontinuous. On the contrary, it is continuous-discontinuous. In this way, a new dimension is given to pedagogy and schools of the future.

Firstly, digital awakening relates to a story (continuous) where adaptation and mastery of technology as a communication form is incorporated and used as a basis (digital literacy). Secondly, instead of clasping onto specific methods, one attempts to surprise and touch the states of slumber (discontinuous) in the hope that the recipient can be awakened to new awareness and insight.

In practice, these will be pedagogical approaches that not only class managers and teachers should use as a basis for their local curricula and lesson plans but they should also be incorporated as principles in national governing documents for schools and education in general. Such transparency is necessary in order to follow the development of terrorism, the way it changes and its instruments, including the use of digital media, which is inherently changing at a rapid pace. Such a fundamental and new form of pedagogy may contribute to the development of a more democratic-oriented type of awareness, including possibilities to uncover and prevent the development of extreme and unforeseen acts.

7

Teaching the Unknown, or How Teachers Can Prepare Students for Uncertainty

Is it possible to prepare the pupils for something that is not yet known?

In this book, we have revolved around the question 'Is it possible to prepare students for something that is not yet known?' Such preparation can not only take place in connection with war, accidents, natural disasters, health and the environment but also events in the classroom or everyday life. The unforeseen is a natural part of life, on a societal and individual level. The consequences can be good or dangerous, and new unforeseen events can arise as a consequence. All people will experience this, to a certain extent, throughout their lives. Training students to handle uncertainty will help to both prepare them personally and better equip society to cope with the unforeseen.

We have also shown that traditional views on learning and teaching planning are not sufficient to handle this type of problem. Didactic models presuppose clear learning goals and internal causal connections between factors, such as goals and content. However, unforeseeable events cannot be controlled or predetermined. The downside of such didactic models is that they lead us into known ways of acting and encourage choices based on past experiences. Rather, planning models must include improvisation and unplanned events. Didactics or the science of teaching must therefore develop new models for planning, that is, models that take account of the unforeseen.

Six actions that can be adapted to the situation and target group

In what follows, we will look at six types of action that teachers and educators can use and adapt in accordance with their target group (Torgersen, 2023; Saeverot & Torgersen, 2024). The actions can take place in different subjects or in interdisciplinary themes from the curriculum.

1. Become familiar with the nature of the unforeseen

Work with the students to develop an understanding of the unforeseen, by examining personal examples and experiences. Based on our teaching experiences, we present practical actions in steps. The intention behind this approach is to provide an overview and clearly demonstrate that each step requires a different level of competence in TU. Moreover, it implies a natural progression in the teaching process. However, it is important to note that these steps can be adjusted and combined, regardless of our stylistic set-up in steps.

Step 1.1. Invest in your own experiences

Find examples, personal or similar, of unexpected events, that is, events with risk and events without risk (or events that were potentially positive).

Step 1.2. Sort the unforeseen events into (1) Risk – (2) No risk

1. Risk: Sort your examples into groups, depending on whether you perceived or experienced them as risks, and whether they were known to you or were unannounced, surprising or sudden.
2. No risk: Sort your experiences that you think did not present any risk or could be an advantage, especially in relation to learning. Divide these events into two groups: experiences that were foreseen and started with signs of warning, and experiences that came unannounced and were completely surprising or sudden.

Step 1.3. Increase awareness of preparation and learning

Exchange the examples and discuss what can be learned from them, while they are happening and afterwards. Discuss how such incidents can be avoided, what kind of preparations can help to mitigate negative effects, and how and what lessons can be used for the future.

2. Familiarize yourself with the nuances of the unforeseen

The unforeseeable is defined as something that occurs relatively unexpectedly and with relatively low probability and predictability for those who experience and handle it (Torgersen, 2018, p. 27). The terms 'relativity' (perspective) and 'time' are important conceptual 'tools' that can be used in the analysis and discussion of experiences to identify nuances in experiences, which in turn can build a feeling of acquirement and ability to act when exposed to new, unforeseen events. Central learning-oriented questions will be: What did I do during a sudden event,? What should I have done differently? What should I do if something new and unpredictable will happen?

Step 2.1. Examine examples and learning potential with regard to the quality 'relativity'

For whom was the event unforeseen? Unforeseeable events depend on the point of view or perspective. An event can be a surprise for some parties (e.g. a community and its emergency services), but can be expected and planned by others (e.g. the terrorist attack on 22 July 2011 on the Norwegian island Utøya and the government quarters in Oslo, or Russia's attack on Ukraine). Unforeseeable events can therefore be objective and concrete, with common experience (and damage) for all involved. But the actual experience of the events can also be subjective. Some will be more robust with regard to psychological effects than others. How robust am I? What kind of events am I normally used to? How can I become more robust? Expectations of unforeseeable events can also be geographically and culturally conditioned:

- A sudden landslide will be more unpredictable in flat areas than in hilly areas.
- Some grow up during war and conflicts where sudden shootings and dangerous incidents are more common than others. This affects both the experience of how unexpected something is expectations and experiences that are important for the handling of the incidents in practice.

By working with these perspectives and questions, one will be able to increase awareness of expectations, degree of self-efficacy and ability to practically handle new unforeseen events.

Step 2.2. Examine examples and learning potential with regard to the quality 'time'

How suddenly did the incident happen? An unforeseeable event can be described in three different time dimensions:

(1) Chronos (chronological time), where the event unfolds in a causal timeline from the first signs of danger (which may or may not be identified, or ignored), perhaps via possible barriers, to the final outcome. This way of thinking means that, objectively speaking, there are no such things as unforeseen events – only warning signals that are not perceived.
(2) Ghost time, where the event is perceived to happen completely suddenly, without any warning. Furthermore, one may experience that the event or the surroundings come towards you, instantly at the same second. An example could be, as previously stated, that you suddenly stumble, without you hardly noticing. Then the experience may be that the floor or the ground is coming towards you, rather than you falling down. Another example could be that you are suddenly surprised by someone scaring you. Then the experience can be that you lose contact with reality and you can feel disoriented and confused.
(3) TU-0 (Unforeseen Time 0) expresses the exact moment when the event occurs, including the immediate aftermath.

All events in the last two dimensions will be perceived as unforeseen – especially in TU-0 – due to their immediacy. Those who live through the event will over time gather more information and connect this to past experiences that can indicate what actually happened. Based on this information, the further development of the incident can be better predicted, and in this way relevant measures can be taken to get out of the situation (recovery). These three time dimensions form the basis for understanding, analysing and discussing one's own experiences, and for developing training scenarios, for unforeseen events. When teaching the students how to react to TU-0, it is important to focus on the ability to capture details during chaos, as a way of keeping the concentration on concurrent learning and sensing the present open.

Step 2.3. Examine examples and learning potential considering the quality of 'continuum fields'

How unknown was the incident? Events can be neither completely unknown nor completely known. All events are to be found in a continuum between these fixed extremes, something we refer to as a continuum field. As a practical exercise, the students can draw on the continuum scale, which shows how an event was experienced to be, in relation to one or more basic structures of the unforeseen, but with only one conceptual category at the time. This experience will in many cases be subjective, but can also be objective, which means that many people experience the same thing, and mark the same place on the scale. When marking, they can do it with a circle or an oblong circle (like a rugby ball), which we call the 'marking ball'. This illustrates that the experience cannot be expressed with a precise point, but rather as a broad area on the scale. One can also create several lines or scales on the same category of the basic structure for the unforeseen, connected to a specific event. In practice, one can 'push' the marking ball back and forth a little, and evaluate the different positions, and see which one fits best with one's own experience.

An unforeseeable event and experience can basically be described in one or more underlying main categories, that is, the degree of:

(1) Relevance (to the target group)
(2) Probability (possibility or chance of occurrence)
(3) How known (in advance of the target group)
(4) Warning signals (scope/number)
(5) Warning time (for given or identified warning signals before an event occurs)
(6) Curiosity (drive to know more)
(7) Wonder (frees oneself from frames and previous truth and understanding, tries to see new things)
(8) Play and create (concretizes ideas and wishes into an action, aesthetic expressions)
(9) Improvisation (letting ideas and coincidences govern, but also conducting repetitions with new meaning and content each time)
(10) Phantasy and imagination (a continuation of wonder, creates completely new solutions and ideas, without connection to the safe framework of reality, or possibilities)

Psychologically, curiosity can be defined as a desire to explore, or acquire knowledge about a phenomenon or an experience (Bjerknes et al., 2023). Curiosity is driven by internal motivation and linked to positive affect in the individual. It is about searching for meaningful knowledge, which leads to an experience of reward and feeling of accomplishment when you reach an answer. Wonder, on the other hand, is about leaving the security we often experience in everyday life behind (Bjerknes et al., 2023). We let habits affect both our thoughts and actions, and we may not spend much energy reflecting so carefully. The starting point for philosophical treatises is very often a question of something that seems like settled knowledge. Here is an example: 'Can I really know that I am sitting and writing this?' Another type of wonder is to ask yourself questions of the type: 'What if?' or 'Why is it so?'

Curiosity is a fundamental internal motivation factor, a driving force, attraction or a desire to gain new experiences and learning, of something in the surroundings, events or situations. Wonder means that you are open to the fact that the world and yourself are different than first thought. It also implies a curiosity to want to explore this. 'Why is it like that?' 'What happens if?' A feeling of great surprise and admiration caused by seeing or experiencing something strange, or new. Common to both definitions of wonder is that it engages us not only intellectually but also emotionally, aesthetically and existentially. Children are often attracted to wonder precisely because wonder is associated with emotions, in particular, good emotions.

All these factors will have different degrees of unforeseeability. They must therefore inform the planning of learning for the unforeseen and can be integrated in exercises and form the basis for the students' analysis of their examples.

3. Put words to feelings and aesthetic forms of expression

All events will affect you in one way or another. Some can be frightening, others positive and uplifting. In order to be as well prepared as possible as to how you experience and cope with unforeseeable events, it is necessary to discuss and put into words your own and other people's feelings. Other forms of expression, such as drawing, dramatization or music, can also be used to articulate experiences where words alone fall short.

An exercise for the students is to describe what kind of feelings were released by certain unforeseen events. At the same time, an awareness-raising method can be to sort the descriptions of the feelings into six groups with main feelings such as these:

- Love
- Happiness
- Surprise
- Anger
- Depression
- Fear

The teacher must always be careful to design progression into the exercises, and monitor with each individual student whether they experience these exercises as good and rich in learning. If the focus turns towards the negative, and creates a bad atmosphere that can have a negative effect on mental health, the teacher should intervene and conduct a dialogue with the student. If this is done early in the process, the exercise can be turned into a positive one, which is the aim of this type of exercise.

4. Make each other good

Social interaction, receiving social support, having trust and developing a sense of accomplishment are the most distinct predictors of being able to handle unforeseen events as best as possible, both for oneself, others and society. Implementing cooperative exercises around the unforeseen is a good thing. Examples of exercises on this can be:

- Encourage the students to give each other extra praise, and to say good words about each other when they work on exercises (e.g. exercises mentioned above).
- Use different forms of communication, for example, verbal, silent and gestures. One reason for this has to do with the fact that dangerous incidents may require different forms of communication, such as silence and gestures.

Providing social support can often be more difficult than you think. It can easily be forgotten when you concentrate on your own tasks and accomplishments. This must therefore be practised. The teacher should observe processes around these exercises, and integrate breaks for comments and reflections, where the social support is either reduced or has been particularly good. Other collaborative exercises for this can be to challenge groups of students with scenarios that contain unforeseen events (in practice). Here are a couple of concrete examples:

- A masked person suddenly enters the classroom during class. How are rehearsed procedures for this carried out? How do we hide; how do we communicate – silently? How can we form a defensive wall in groups?
- Similar collaborative exercises can be done during exercises for fire, earthquake, landslide and others – preferably scenarios that are progressively different, always with new elements and with an increasing degree of unfamiliarity (and other factors such as warning signals and warning time – see Step 2.3).

All exercises must be followed by reflections and debriefings, where practical interaction is the focus.

5. Make sure that the theme 'the unforeseen' is included in the curricula

This systematic educational work to prepare the students for uncertainty should be carried out in stages and given sufficient time. Exercises can be done several times during the year. New unforeseen events will continue to happen, and as the students become more familiar with the phenomenon and the concept of the unforeseen, they will be able to identify it more precisely, get better routines for how they can handle it and thus continuously learn more and be better prepared. A school must coordinate this across different grade levels and subjects to ensure clear progression and continuity. The unforeseen as a theme can be included in all subjects or organized as an interdisciplinary project. Learning about the unforeseen can, for example, be a natural part of the school's theme linked to sustainability, democracy and mental health. In order to achieve systematic training, this should be described in the school's curricula, with an overview of the knowledge, learning objectives, working methods, progression, coordination between subjects and also evaluation forms (Saeverot & Torgersen, 2022). An important point here is that these overviews must be flexible and connected to the nature of the unforeseen. Improvisation and spontaneity in learning plans and pedagogical practices are therefore important in order to grasp new learning opportunities as they arise.

6. Adopt existential communication

In our time, the school's main focus should perhaps not be to add more knowledge to the students, as they are already inundated with knowledge through the internet. We have also seen, among other things, that a heavy focus on knowledge easily leads to academic pressure on children and young people and the unfortunate consequences that this can entail. As a response to this development which largely values predictability, we have proposed that there should be a greater focus on unpredictability, such as existence, subjectivity, passion, emotions as well as strengthening the students' ability to assess the quality of all the information and knowledge that we all have such easy access to, especially through our smartphones. In order to achieve this in schools, there must be room for existential communication, where the direct and indirect aspects are not separate categories. The direct and indirect are rather to be found in a continuum, where they derive from each other. Having said that, the indirect aspect, especially due to its unpredictability, has a stronger impact than the direct and controlling aspect when it comes to unforeseen topics such as existence. It is also related to the fact that the indirect aspect has better precision, that is to say that it can easily hit 'the nerve' that causes reflection. On the other hand, indirect communication, like anything else, can be abused by those who use it. That is why it is utmost important that those who make use of indirectness have good intentions and know what they are doing, so as to prevent manipulation and hidden indoctrination.

References

Aumann, A. (2019). Kierkegaard on the Value of Art: An Indirect Method of Communication. In A. Buben, E. Helms & P. Stokes (Eds.), *The Kierkegaardian Mind* (pp. 166–76). Routledge.

Austeng, K., Torp, O., Midtbø, J. T., Helland, V. & Jordanger, I. (2005). *Usikkerhetsanalyse – Metoder [Analysis of Uncertainty – Methods]*. Concept rapport, no. 12. NTNU/Institutt for bygg, anlegg og transport, Conceptprogrammet.

Aven, T. (2014). *Risk, Surprises and Black Swans*. Routledge.

Baldacchino, J. (2019). *Art as Unlearning. Towards a Mannerist Pedagogy*. Routledge.

Bammer, G. & Smithson, M. (Eds.) (2008). *Uncertainty and Risk: Multidisciplinary Perspectives*. Routledge.

Barnett, R. (2004). Learning for an Unknown Future. *Higher Education Research & Development*, 23(3), 247–60. https://admin.hv.se/globalassets/dokument/stodja/paper-theme-2-5.pdf.

Beck, U. (1992). *Risk Society, towards a New Modernity*. Sage Publications.

Bernstein, B. & og Saloman, J. (1999). Pedagogy, Identity and the Construction of a Theory of Symbolic Control. Basil Bernstein Questioned by Joseph Soloman. *British Journal of Sociology of Education*, 20(2), 265–79.

Biesta, G. (2014). *The Beautiful Risk of Education*. Paradigm Publishers.

Biesta, G. (2015). Å kreve det umulige» – å arbeide med det uforutsette i utdanningen [«Demanding the Impossible» – To Work with the Unforeseen in Education]. In G.-E. Torgersen (Ed.), *Pedagogikk for det uforutsette [Pedagogy for the Unforeseen]* (pp. 273–82). Fagbokforlaget.

Bjerknes, A.-L., Wilhelmsen, T. & Foyn-Bruun, E. (2023). A Systematic Review of Curiosity and Wonder in Natural Science and Early Childhood Education Research. *Journal of Research in Childhood Education*, 50–65. https://doi.org/10.1080/02568543.2023.2192249.

Bjørndal, B. & Lieberg, S. (1978). *Nye veier i didaktikken? [New Paths in Didactics?]*. Aschehoug.

Black, P. & Wiliam, D. (2009). Developing the Theory of Formative Assessment. *Educational Assessment, Evaluation and Accountability*, 21(1), 5–31.

114   References

Bollnow, O. F. (1959/1977). *Existenzphilosophie und Pädagogik. Versuch über unstetige Formen der Erziehung.* W. Kohlhammer.

Bollnow, O. F. (1969). *Eksistensfilosofi og pedagogikk* [Existential Philosophy and Pedagogy]. Fabritius & Sønners forlag.

Currie, M. (2013). *The Unexpected. Narrative Temporality and the Philosophy of Surprise.* Edinburgh University Press Ltd.

Darsø, L. (2012). *Innovationspædagogik. Kunsten at fremelske innovationskompetence* [Innovation Pedagogy. The Art of Promoting Innovation Competence]. Samfundslitteratur.

Derrida, J. (1994). *Specters of Marx.* Routledge.

Djikic, M. & Oatley, K. (2014). The Art of Fiction: From Indirect Communication to Changes in the Self. *Psychology of Aesthetics, Creativity, and the Arts,* 8(4), 498–505.

EFG-BN (2011). Video. Retrieved 10 November 2011, from http://efg-bnusfoodreserves.blogspot.com/2011/07/video-drsteve-pieczenik-breivik-oslo.html.

Espeland, Å. (2022). *Didaktisk improvisasjon i musikkundervisning – ein studie av undervisningspraksisar i kulturskule og ungdomsskule* [Didactic Improvisation in Music Education – A Study of Teaching Practices in Culture Schools and Secondary Schools]. PhD thesis, University of Bergen.

Fimreite, A. L., Lango, P., Lægreid, P. & Hellebø Rykkja, L. (Eds.) (2014). *Organisering, samfunnssikkerhet og krisehåndtering* [Organisation, Social Security and Crisis Management]. Universitetsforlaget.

Fraser, B. & Brown, W. (in press, 2024). Toward an Understanding of Teaching through Indirect Communication. In J. Baldacchino & H. Saeverot (Eds.), *The Bloomsbury Handbook of Continental Philosophy of Education.* Bloomsbury.

Gary, K. (2007). Kierkegaard and Liberal Education as a Way of Life. *Philosophy of Education Archive,* 63(1), 151–8. https://doi.org/10.47925/2007.151.

Herberg, M. (2022). *Competence for the Unforeseen: The importance of individual, social and organizational factors.* Doctoral theses at NTNU, 2022:236. Faculty of Social and Educational Sciences. Trondheim.

Holdhus, K., Høisæter, S., Mæland, K., Vangsnes, V., Engelsen, K. S., Espeland, M. & Espeland, Å. (2016). Improvisation in Teaching and Education – Roots and Applications. *Cogent Education,* 3(1), 1–17. https://doi.org/10.1080/2331186X.2016.1204142.

Hollnagel, E. (2016). *Resilience Engineering.* Retrieved from https://erikhollnagel.com/ideas/resilience-engineering.html.

Hollnagel, E., Woods, D. D. & Leveson, N. C. (Eds.) (2006). *Resilience Engineering: Concepts and Precepts.* Ashgate.

Hollnagel, E., Pariés, J., Woods, D. & Wreathall, J. (2010). *Resilience Engineering in Practice: A Guidebook*. CRC Press, Taylor & Francis Group.

Hopmann, S. (2010). Undervisningens avgrensning: didaktikkens kjerne [*Demarcation of Teaching: The Core of Didactics*]. In J. H. Midtsundstad & I. Willbergh (Eds.), *Didaktikk. Nye teoretiske perspektiver på undervisning* [*Didactics. New Theoretical Perspectives on Teaching*] (pp. 19–45). Cappelen Akademiske forlag.

Karlsen, G. (2006). Stilt overfor det som ennå ikke er [Faced with What Is Not Yet]. In K. Steinsholt & H. Sommerro (Eds.), *Improvisasjon. Kunsten å sette seg selv på spill* [*Improvisation. The Art of Putting Yourself on the Line*] (pp. 239–59). N.W. Damm & Søn AS.

Kierkegaard, S. (1978). Synspunktet for min Forfatter-Virksomhed [*The Point of View* of My Work as an Author], volume 18. In A. B. Drachmann, J. L. Heiberg & H. Ostenfeldt Lange (Eds.), *Søren Kierkegaard: Samlede Værker* [*Søren Kierkegaard: Collected Works*], volume 1–20. Gyldendal.

Kristensen, J. E. (2017). Samtidsdiagnostik, videnspolitik og kritik. Med særligt henblik på uddannelse og uddannelsesvidenskab [Contemporary Diagnoses, Science Policy and Criticism. With a Particular Focus on Education and Educational Sciences]. In A. K. Ljungdalh, J. A. Lysgaard & O. Tafdrup (Eds.), *Uddannelsesvidenskab – en kritisk introduktion* [*Educational Sciences – A Critical Introduction*] (pp. 15–50). Samfundslitteratur.

Kristensen, J. E. (2022). Pædagogik og/eller uddannelsesforskning og uddannelsesvidenskab? Danske konstellationer og spændinger [Pedagogy and/or Educational Research and Educational Sciences? Danish Constellations and Tensions]. *Nordic Studies in Education*, 42(1), 30–49. https://doi.org/10.23865/nse.v42.3796.

Künzli, R. (1998). The Common Frame and the Places of Didaktik. In B. B. Gundem & S. Hopmann (Eds.), *Didaktik and/or Curriculum: An International Dialogue* (pp. 29–45). P. Lang.

Kvernbekk, T., Torgersen, G.-E. & Moe, I. (2015). Om begrepet det uforutsette [On the Concept of the Unforeseen]. In G.-E. Torgersen (Ed.), *Pedagogikk for det uforutsette* [*Pedagogy for the Unforeseen*] (pp. 28–56). Fagbokforlaget.

Loeng, S., Torgersen, G.-E., Melbye, P. E. & Lodgaard, E. (2001). *Voksenpedagogikk i kompetansesamfunnet* [*Adult Education in the Competence Society*]. Læringsforlaget.

Løgstrup, K. E. (2000). *Den etiske fordring* [*The Ethical Demand*]. Cappelen.

Lunde, I. K. (2014). *Praktisk krise- og beredskapsledelse* [*Practical Crisis and Emergency Management*]. Universitetsforlaget.

Mason, J. & Spence, M. (1999). Beyond Mere Knowledge of Mathematics: The Importance of Knowing-to Act in the Moment. *Educational Studies in Mathematics*, 38(1–3), 135–61.

Mitroff, I. I., Alpaslan, M. C. & Green, S. E. (2004). Crises as Ill-Structured Messes. *International Studies Review*, 6(1), 165–94.

Montuori, A. (2003). The Complexity of Improvisation and the Improvisation of Complexity: Social Science, Art and Creativity. *Human Relations*, 56(2), 237–55. https://doi.org/10.1177/0018726703056002893.

Mueller, J. (2012). Six Rather Unusual Propositions about Terrorism. In J. Horgan & K. Braddock (Eds.), *Terrorism Studies. A Reader* (pp. 403–19). Routledge.

Myrstad, A. & Sverdrup, T. (2009). Improvisasjon – et verktøy for å forstå de yngste barnas medvirkning i barnehagen? [Improvisation – A Tool for Understanding the Participation of the Youngest Children in the Kindergarten?]. *BARN*, 27(2), 51–68. https://doi.org/10.5324/barn.v27i2.4284.

Nemeth, C. & Hollnagel, E. (2014). *Resilience Engineering in Practice, Volume 2: Becoming Resilient* (Ashgate Studies in Resilience Engineering). CRC Press, Taylor & Francis Group.

Nielsen, A. B. (2014). *Hatprat [Hate Speech]*. Cappelen Damm.

Nonaka, I., Toyama, R. & Konno, N. (2000). SECI, Ba and Leadership: A Unified Model of Dynamic Knowledge Creation. *Long Range Planning*, 33, 5–34.

Oddane, T. (2015). Improvisasjon – en nøkkel til rytmisk smidig beredskap overfor det uforutsette [Improvisation – A Key to Rhythmically Flexible Readiness for the Unforeseen]. In G.-E. Torgersen (Ed.), *Pedagogikk for det uforutsette [Pedagogy for the Unforeseen]* (pp. 232–62). Fagbokforlaget.

Peters, M. (2008). Education and Security in the Age of Terrorism: 'The Battle for Young Minds'. In T. Kvernbekk, H. Simpson & M. A. Peters (Eds.), *Military Pedagogies. And Why They Matters* (pp. 180–2). Sense Publishers.

Rausand, M. (2014). *Reliability of Safety-Critical Systems: Theory and Applications*. Wiley-Blackwell.

Reier Jensen, A. (2016). *En dialektisk studie av formaliserte veiledningssamtaler i lærerutdanningens praksisperiode [A Dialectical Study of Formalised Supervision in the Practical Period of Teacher Education]*. PhD thesis, University of Agder.

Rescher, N. (1998). *Predicting the Future. An Introduction to the Theory of Forecasting*. State University of New York Press.

Ripley, A. (2009). *The Unthinkable: Who Survives When Disaster Strikes*. Random House/Three Rivers Press.

Roberts, P. & Saeverot, H. (2018). *Education and the Limits of Reason. Reading Dostoevsky, Tolstoy and Nabokov*. Routledge.

Saeverot, H. (2011). Kierkegaard, Seduction, and Existential Education. *Studies in Philosophy and Education*, 30(6), 557–72.

Saeverot, H. (2013). *Indirect Pedagogy: Some Lessons in Existential Education*. Sense Publishers.

Saeverot, H. (2018). Invisible Teaching. In P. Smeyers (Ed.), *International Handbook of Philosophy of Education*, Part 1 (pp. 243–57). Springer.

Saeverot, H. (Ed.) (2022a). *Meeting the Challenges of Existential Threats through Educational Innovation: A Proposal for an Expanded Curriculum*. Routledge.

Saeverot, H. (2022b). *Indirect Education: Exploring Indirectness in Teaching and Research*. Routledge.

Saeverot, H. & Kristensen, J. E. (2022). Introduksjon: Pedagogikk under press. Hvordan kan vi motstå presset? [Introduction: Pedagogy under Pressure. How Can We Resist the Pressure?]. *Nordic Studies in Education*, 42(1), 1–12. https://doi.org/10.23865/nse.v42.3784.

Saeverot, H. & Torgersen, G.-E. (2022). SSE-Based Frame of Reference. Outlines for a Global Curriculum: Turning Existential Threats into Resources. In H. Saeverot (Ed.), *Meeting the Challenges of Existential Threats through Educational Innovation: A Proposal for an Expanded Curriculum* (pp. 11–26). Routledge.

Saeverot, H. & Torgersen, G.-E. (2024). *Undervisning for det uføreseielege* [*Teaching for the Unforeseen*]. Samlaget.

Sawyer, R. K. (2011). *Structure and Improvisation in Creative Teaching*. Cambridge University Press.

Sheffi, Y. (2005). *The Resilient Enterprise: Overcoming Vulnerability for Competitive Advantage*. MIT Press.

Sheffi, Y. (2017). *The Power of Resilience: How the Best Companies Manage the Unexpected*. MIT Press.

Smith, James K. A. (2009). *Desiring the Kingdom: Worship, Worldview, and Cultural Formation. Cultural Liturgies 1*. Baker.

Steinsholt, K. & Sommerro, H. (Eds.) (2006). *Improvisasjon. Kunsten å sette seg selv på spill* [*Improvisation. The Art of Putting Yourself on the Line*]. N.W. Damm & Søn AS.

Taleb, N. N. (2010/2007). *The Black Swan: The Impact of the Highly Improbable*. Penguin.

References

Taylor, M. & Horgan, J. (2012). *A Conceptual Framwork for Addressing Psychological Process in the Development of the Terrorist.* In J. Horgan & K. Braddock (Eds.), *Terrorism Studies. A Reader* (pp. 130–43). Routledge.

Tetlock, P. E. & Gardner, D. (2015). *Superforecasting – The Art and Science of Prediction.* Crown Publishers.

Torgersen, G.-E. (2008). The Idea of a Military Pedagogical Doctrine. In T. Kvernbekk, H. Simpson & M. A. Peters (Eds.), *Military Pedagogies. And Why They Matters* (pp. 43–62). Sense Publishers.

Torgersen, G.-E. (Ed.) (2015). *Pedagogikk for det uforutsette [Pedagogy for the Unforeseen].* Fagbokforlaget.

Torgersen, G.-E. (Ed.) (2018). *Interaction: 'Samhandling' under Risk – A Step Ahead of the Unforeseen.* Cappelen Damm Akademiske, Nordic Open Access Scholarly Publishing (NOASP). https://press.nordicopenaccess.no/index.php/noasp/catalog/book/36.

Torgersen, G.-E. (2023). Teaching the Unknown: How to Prepare Students for Uncertainty. *Times Higher Education.* https://www.timeshighereducation.com/campus/teaching-unknown-how-prepare-students-uncertainty.

Torgersen, G.-E. & Saeverot, H. (2011). *Bildung and the Pictorial Turn – Or, the Future of Bildung in the Image Society.* The 41st Annual Conference of the Philosophy of Education Society of Australasia Inc.

Torgersen, G.-E. & Saeverot, H. (2012). Danningens nye ansikt i risikosamfunnet – digital vekking mot virtuell terrorisme [The New Face of Formation in the Risk Society – Digital Awakening towards Virtual Terrorism]. *Norsk Filosofisk Tidsskrift,* 47(3), 170–9.

Torgersen, G.-E. & Saeverot, H. (2015). Strategisk didaktisk modell for det uforutsette [Strategic Didactic Model for the Unforeseen]. In G.-E. Torgersen (Ed.), *Pedagogikk for det uforutsette [Pedagogy for the Unforeseen]* (pp. 317–38). Fagbokforlaget.

Torgersen, G.-E., Steiro, T. & Saeverot, H. (2015). Den fjerde vei – indirekte danning mot det uforutsette [The Fourth Way – Indirect Education towards the Unforeseen]. In G.-E. Torgersen (Ed.), *Pedagogikk for det uforutsette [Pedagogy for the Unforeseen]* (pp. 297–309). Fagbokforlaget.

Trygsland, G. (2017). *Hva kjennetegner grammatikkundervisningen i tre norske klasserom? En kvalitativ videostudie [What Characterizes Grammar Teaching in Three Norwegian Classrooms? A Qualitative Video Study].* Master thesis, University of Oslo.

Weick, K. E. & Sutcliffe, K. M. (2015). *Managing the Unexpected: Sustained Performance in a Complex World.* Wiley.

Index

actor terrorists 91
aesthetic forms of expression 45–8, 109–10
Anglo-American curriculum tradition 14
Annual Threat Assessment of the U.S. Intelligence Community 19
anthropogenic climate change 41

'Ba,' concept of 25
Bammer, G. 32
  Uncertainty and Risk – Multidisciplinary Perspectives 24
Barnett, R., *Learning for an Unknown Future* 33
Beck, U. viii. *See also* risk(s), society
behavioural communication 44
Bernstein, B. 18
Biesta, G., risk of education 87
black swans 10, 23
  in finance 24
Bollnow, O. F. 54–5, 67–9, 101
  characteristics/prerequisites for awakening 98–9
  educational awakening 97
  existence-oriented pedagogy 54–5
  Existenzphilosophie und Pädagogik. Versuch über unstetige Formen der Erziehung 96

chronos (chronological time) 106
climate change 26, 41, 46
communication 9, 19, 75, 93, 98. *See also* forms of communication
  behavioural 44

existential (*see* existential communication)
predictable and unpredictable forms of 41–5
Conspiracy 46
Continental European pedagogical didactic theory 14
continuous and discontinuous awakening
  from digital slumber 96–7
  insight and problem of continuity 97–9
continuum fields 74, 107–9
Crash 48
curiosity 108
curriculum theory ix, 30–1
Currie, M., *The Unexpected. Narrative Temporality and the Philosophy of Surprise* 34

danger signals and prevention viii, 10, 13–14, 17
Danningens nye ansikt i risikosamfunnet (*The New Face of Education in the Risk Society*) 34
Darsø, L. 76
  'Diamond of Innovation' 82
  knowledge and non-knowledge 76
deeper forms of learning 29
Derrida, J. 54
  hauntology 54, 57–60
  Specters of Marx 57, 59, 60–1
Didactic Balance Model (DBM model) 71, 87–9
  curricula 90
  harmony and diversity 89–90

pedagogical practice 90
political goals 89
didactic models 71, 103
 Bow-tie model 11–12, 71, 74
 challenging traditional models 17
 and teaching principles, new
  17–19
didactic perspectives 16
didactic problem 31
didactics of language 54
didactic triangle 51–2
digital attacks 91
digital awakening
 continuous and discontinuous
  awakening 96–9
 problem 96
 schools of future 102
 sensible vigilance and 91–2
 terrorism's rate of change 92–4
 through exegetic approaches 100
 through indirect pedagogy 101
 virtual terrorism 94–5
digital media 91, 102
digital slumber 96–7
digital social media 14
direct form of communication 48–9

educational theory of the unforeseen
 (EdTU) 17, 20–1
Eichmann, A. 47
existence-oriented pedagogy 54–6
existential communication 42–3,
 49–50, 112
 predictable and unpredictable
  communication 43–5
existential education 39
experience, TU 8–9
experiential learning and TU 14, 31–2

forecasting theory, superforecasting
 vs. 24–5
foreseen 17, 44, 63, 72
foresight 3, 10, 29, 31, 48, 84, 94–5,
 97–102

formal education 54
forms of communication 39, 44,
 101–2, 110
 art and literature as indirect 48
 direct 48–9
 indirect 48–9, 64–5, 112
 predictable and unpredictable
  41–5
 unlearning and aesthetic forms
  45–7
Fosse, J., *Aliss at the Fire* 57

Gardner, D., *Superforecasting –
 the Art and Science of
 Prediction* 24
Ghostbusters 59
ghost hunting 59
ghost time 58, 106
 and improvisation 61–7
global-economic concepts 37

hauntology 54, 57–60
Heydrich, R. 47–8
High Reliability Organizations
 (HRO) systems 25
Hollnagel, E. 27
 essence of resilience 28
 *Resilience Engineering:
  Concepts and Precepts*
  27–8
Humboldt, F. H. A. 54
Hume, D. 23
hybrid threats (HT) 91

Ibsen, H., *Ghosts* 57
ignorance and naivety 45
improvisation 51–2
 as 'believing in ghosts'/'seeing
  more than we do' 56–61
 definitions 55–6
 disciplined 56
 ghost time and 61–7
 music and didactic 64
 problems and questions 53–5

risk (*Wagnis*) and failure 67–70
  and spontaneity 112
  spontaneous 66–7
  and unforeseen 52–3
indirect communication 48–9, 64–5, 112
indirect pedagogy 19, 33, 100, 102
  digital awakening through 101
  and unpredictable teaching aids 48
interaction 30, 75–6, 110
Interaction: Under Risk – A Step Ahead of the Unforeseen 34
internet generation (iGen) 94, 97–8

Kierkegaard, S. 41–2
knowledge 2, 4, 19, 45–6, 54, 86, 93, 98, 100, 108, 111–12
  attainment 41
  and existence 42
  and non-knowledge 76
  to plans 30–1
  society 37
    ignorance of 38–9
  and theory ix
'Knowledge Competency' 82–3
knowledge economy
  development 49
  regime 39–41
knowledge structures
  interactions 30
  learning, training and 29–30
  system *vs.* 28–9
Kritzinger, F. 46–8

Lange, R. 47
learning objectives 9, 17, 51, 76, 81, 86
learning theory ix
Løgstrup, K. E. 68
looming crisis 73

main goal 43–4
Marshall Plan 37, 49
moments of contingency 56
multidisciplinary approach 24

Nemeth, C. 28
'No Knowledge' 83–5
Nonaka, I. 25
Norwegian curriculum 41–2
Norwegian Ministry of Education and Research 19

Organisation for Economic Co-operation and Development (OECD) 37, 37 n.1
organizational learning 25–6
organizational research 25

pedagogical approach 76, 93, 101–2
pedagogical goals
  main goal 43–4
  sub-goal 43–4
pedagogical practice ix, 51–3, 57, 67, 88–90, 112
pedagogical science 31, 33
pedagogy 2–3, 9, 16, 20, 39, 44, 49, 53–4, 64, 66, 77, 92–3, 96, 102
Pedagogy for the Unforeseen (TUPED) 33–5
Peters, M. A. 93
Philosophy of Education Society of Australasia Inc. 33
Pieczenik, S. R. 94
planning instruction and training 16
political-economic pedagogy 39
Popper, K., white swans 23
predictions 24–5
preparedness ix, 2–3, 8, 14, 52, 54, 74–6, 81, 83, 87, 91
  and crisis management 3
  organizational 25
  research 54

racism 48
Rausand, M., *Reliability of Safety-Critical Systems: Theory and Applications* 28

relative, TU 8, 72
relativity 105
Rescher, N., *Predicting the Future. An Introduction to the Theory of Forecasting* 25
research 24, 71
  focus and goals 12–13
  improvisation 53
  learning, training and knowledge structures 29–30
  in Norway 33
  organizational 25
  and publications 34–5
  resilience 26–7
  system *vs.* knowledge structures 28–9
  TU *vs.* 31
  theory development and 11–12
  traditional risk 26, 31
  TU Group 32–3
resilience 26
  definitions of 27–8
  in organizations 27
  research 26–7
  system *vs.* knowledge structures 28–9
  TU *vs.* 31
  societal 28
  thinking 11
reverse didactic degree 86–7
Ripley, A., *The Unthinkable: Who Survives When Disaster Strikes* 28
risk(s) 25, 68–9, 73, 104
  of education 87
  improvisation 67–70
  management 74
  nuanced differences in expression (TU) 5–7
  and risk analyses 24
  society viii, 2, 19, 93
  traditional risk research 26, 31

Saeverot, H. 87
  Meeting the Challenges of Existential Threats through Educational Innovation. A Proposal for an Expanded Curriculum 34–5
Sawyer, R. K. 53
school(s) viii, 49, 92, 96, 100, 111–12
  digital literacy of pupils 95
  and education 3, 14, 37, 53, 78, 89, 93, 102
  forms of communication 44
  of future 102
  lesson, unpredictability and possibilities 15–16
self-knowledge 44–5
self-reflection 43, 48, 98
sensible vigilance 91–2
Shakespeare, W., *Hamlet* 57, 58
Sheffi, Y. 27
  The Power of Resilience: How the Best Companies Manage the Unexpected 27
  The Resilient Enterprise: Overcoming Vulnerability for Competitive Advantage 27
Smithson, M., *Uncertainty and Risk – Multidisciplinary Perspectives* 24
social media 14, 38, 46, 91, 96–9, 101
social support 110
societal developments 16, 20
societal resilience 28
sociopolitical background and current affairs 19
Sommerro, H. 53
spontaneous improvisation 66–7
spontaneous utilization of harmless unforeseen 16
Spranger, E. 101
Steinsholt, K. 53
Stoltenberg, J. 91, 93

Strategic didactic model for The
 Unforeseen (SD-TU
 model) 71, 75-8
 competency structures 81, 82-3
 'Knowledge Competency'
  82-3
 'No Knowledge' 84-5
 'Tiers of Unforeseeability' 85
 content and meaning 78-80
 critical use of 86-7
 Diamond Model of Crisis
  Management: Interactive
  Systems Thinking 77
 known competencies 81-3
 main principles and concepts of
  model 78, 81
 relation model for adult education
  76-7
 traditional 'part' and 'tu-oriented
  learning habits' 81
 unknown 83-6
strategic pedagogical problem 3
Strindberg, A., *The Ghost Sonata* 57
sub-goal 43-4
subjectivity and unpredictability
 44-5
sudden crisis 73
superforecasting *vs.* theory of
 forecasting 24-5
sustainable pedagogy 90
Sutcliffe, K., *Managing the
 Unexpected: Sustained
 Performance in a Complex
 World* 25

Taleb, N. N., *The Black Swan: The
 Impact of the Highly
 Improbable* 24
target audience and examples 20
target group 104-12
terrorism 98, 102
 rate of change 92-4
 virtual 94-5

Tetlock, P., *Superforecasting – the Art
 and Science of Prediction* 24
theory and model development 12
tiers of unforeseeability 73, 84-5
time and unforeseen 14, 18-19,
 105-7
Torgersen, G.-E. 87
 Pedagogikk for det uforutsette
  (Pedagogy for
  the unforeseen,
  Fagbokforlaget) 34
total foreseen/unforeseen 72
traditional curriculum theory ix
traditional models, challenging 17
traditional risk research 26, 31
TU-0 (Unforeseen Time 0) 9-11,
 106-7
TU Group 32-3
TU-oriented learning habits 81
'TU Relations' 83
TU symposium
 Akershus Fortress, Oslo (2014) 34
 at House of Literature, Bergen
  (2019) 34

unexpectedness 73, 86
unforeseeability 4, 68, 103, 105, 109
 tiers of 73, 84-5
unforeseen (TU) viii-ix, 1, 3, 23-4,
 44, 72, 103
 awareness of preparation and
  learning 105
 characteristics 8-10
 conditions 52
 in curricula 111
 definition 1
 degree of 74-5
 didactic perspectives 16
 experiences 104
 experiential learning and 31-2
 goal 2
 nuanced differences in 3-7
 nuances of 105-9

relation and continuum 72–4
risk and no risk 104
time and 14, 18–19
time dimensions 106–7
unpredictability 8, 10, 18, 25, 40, 87, 112
  forms of communication 41–5
  indirectness and 50
  and possibilities of school lesson 15–16
  subjectivity and 44–5
  teaching aids 48

unpreparedness 74
unwanted incidents 26, 28, 32, 52, 74

virtual terrorism 94–5

Wagnis 67–9
Wannsee Conference (Berlin) 46
weak education process 88
Weick, K. E., *Managing the Unexpected: Sustained Performance in a Complex World* 25